FATHERS AND SONS:
IN AND ABOUT EDUCATION

To Sue.
With thanks for
your support
Love.
Philip
x

FATHERS AND SONS:
IN AND ABOUT EDUCATION

Philip Garner and
Peter Clough

Trentham Books
Stoke on Trent, UK and Sterling, USA

Trentham Books Limited
Westview House 22883 Quicksilver Drive
734 London Road Sterling
Oakhill VA 20166-2012
Stoke on Trent USA
Staffordshire
England ST4 5NP

First published 2008

British Library Cataloguing-in-Publication Data
A catalogue record for this book is available from the British Library

ISBN: 978 1 85856 370 1

Designed and typeset by Trentham Print Design Ltd., Chester and printed in Great Britain by Cromwell Press Ltd, Wiltshire.

Contents

Dedication

To Fathers and Sons everywhere, but especially to James Edward Garner.
And Charlie Theodore, Keir Gabriel, and of course, to Jimmy.
To them, 'Long may you run...'

Acknowledgements

A number of people need ... deserve ... to be thanked for their conscious or unwitting contributions to this book, including 'our' fathers and sons: Gerry, Ian, Ally, Tom, Mike, Ronnie, Wilf, Merv, Richard, Ramzi, Gary, Mark, Evan, Steve, Lee(1), Michael, David, Salim, Iain, Tony, Kevin, Lee(2), Wes, Marvin and William. Their surnames are omitted – they know who they are

We would also like to extend our gratitude to colleagues in our respective university departments, and those in partner institutions and schools, who have variously made inputs to this book along the way. As is customary, any shortcomings are not theirs but those of the authors.

Finally, the elongated gestation of this book has been supported, even indulged, by Gillian Klein of Trentham Books; her enthusiasm for the project, together with considerable forbearance, has largely been responsible for bringing this book to fruition. Grateful thanks.

1

Introduction, rationale and orientation

'I could tell you all about being a Dad. From both sides, I could do that. But you'll need to have a few spare hours on your hands' [A]

We suppose that you might be expecting a post-modern, Foucauldian critique? But let's instead strip things down to the real lives of those who live as Dads or 'Fathers'. And the corresponding real lives of their sons, most of whom will surely become fathers themselves. They all – these fathers and their sons – live deep this rich, intellectualised snobbery, for that's what it is, in all its now vainglorious, withering and hollow post-Research Assessment Exercise posturing. Fortunately these fathers and their sons experience a real life beyond that which the academy bestows on them. What passes as real life in a kind of Warhol-captured minute in the minds of many head-in the-sand educational researchers is not what we're about to present. Could we be more preposterous than to present this stuff, this heart-and-soul roulette-wheel that frequently characterises our narrative, as 'research'?

This book is not about objective 'research', 'hypotheses', 'data' or findings. We are both far too close to living as fathers and sons ourselves to claim neutrality or independence. It describes, in the words of these Fathers and Sons and of two participant-researchers a new notion of an individual 'researching' the product of the act of procreation! It's about the experiences of boys and men who have lived and are living through difficult times as 'others' in this increasingly and sometimes pointlessly gendered phase of human development.

Neither is this an 'academic' book – a term which allows only for structured competence and a careful balance of argument and counter-argument. There is, it seems to us, a danger of an absence of soul in the service of a 'truth'. In considering the lives of fathers and sons such an omission is a potential disaster. It risks further reducing the act of fathering, and of being a son, to a mundane and passionless process. And that, we believe, will cause 'good fathers' to become tragedies. Our argument throughout this volume is that fathers and sons inhabit a singular, emotional territory which is not well served by quantification. We seek to critically interrogate the roles played by fathers and sons in this book, and to celebrate their journeys and rejoice in their outcomes at whichever level they reach or in whatever arena they perform.

As part of that celebration we intended not to over-interpret the meanings of the words that our father and son narrators use to convey their experiences. Elsewhere (Clough and Garner, 2001) we have argued that there is, at a fundamental level in the ethical frame around which all research is constructed, a need to retain collections of words as they emerge. Researchers ought really to view these data as sacrosanct: to merge, delete, juxtapose or abbreviate them is a failure of researcher integrity. It butchers the structure and natural rhythm that makes these utterances the belongings of the respondent and consequently loses meaning.

In this book we have not attempted to be systematic either in our choice of topics and the materials which illustrate them, or in an analysis of these issues and phenomena. Our selection and organisation has been led quite deliberately by experiences we have found in our own lives – as both teachers and researchers – to be not unusual in the lives of those we have taught and with whom we have made data. The phrase 'in our own lives' is emphasised, because whilst we may write as and for teachers and researchers, a regressed aspect of our identities is sometimes given voice here. These are some of our own experiences as sons and fathers and we hope this speaks to our readers, whether male or female.

We have both worked with aspects of special educational needs (SEN), inclusion and disability for most of our educational careers, firstly in schools and units and more recently in higher education, contributing to initial teacher education, continuing professional development and research. In these roles and posts we have probably seen some of the more extreme forms and expressions of father/son relationships: fathers who are on the edge, marginalised or played out. Children broken by broken parents and by support systems which are depleted of resource. And both fathers and sons are sometimes broken too by withering cycles of deprivation and emotional starvation or abuse.

So we have an abiding interest in the lives of boys and men with whom we have made connections in various ways and at various times, and who signpost the territory of things that are termed 'special' in education. In consequence, some readers may come to view this collection as representing neither the boyhoods nor fatherings with which they are familiar. We write here about some of the marginalised life experiences of fathers and sons. But we also recognise that they do not always represent the ordinary experiences characterised by being actualised, grounded and inhabited by secure emotions, relationships and futures. These chapters, with their informing data, are our own personal and professional fragments, used in ways which we hope will highlight the tension, expectations and sometimes disappointments that define the life and times of a significant minority of fathers and sons.

Our own experiences of SEN and disabilities are important for a second reason: you cannot work for long with a range of labels and groupings without realising that such categorisations frequently mask the lived experiences of those who are ordered, sifted and grouped. So whilst they may usefully describe behaviours, they can seldom relate to experiences; and whilst categories may be used in this way to characterise particular populations, homogeneity is not being brought to the members of a labelled group.

We are all to be found somewhere along the continua which are too often seen as exclusive categorisations. There are fathers and sons who encounter extreme difficulties in their lives. But it is important not to regard them as different people or species, or think that their generic experiences, though often stressed, are inconsistent with those of other fathers and sons. In this book we focus on father and son relationships which we have grouped for the purpose of cohesion. That these loose groupings relate most frequently to marginalised fathering should not deflect us from seeing them, both men and boys, as just like 'us'.

We talk variously in this book as fathers and as sons. We sometimes use our own data, recalling moments in our childhoods, our fathering careers or in our work involvement with young people and their dads. And we use that of other fathers and their sons. These data are messy and miscellaneous. In one sense they may in themselves be a metaphor for being a father: sometimes inconsistent and chaotic, always 'needed' and yet at other times better left to idle on the side. And our data, illustrating as it does some of the themes we seek to address, comprise fact and fictions. We do not claim these data as representative or generalisable. But they are central to the spirit of this book. We present in various formats our picked-over impressions of being sons and fathers. They are fauvist sketches of our emotions, splattering and splashing their primary-coloured intensity across the reader's canvas whilst illustrating the theoretical, conceptual and experiential domains of fathers and sons. And there are no edges to these narratives – they do not have endings, nor can they be viewed as fixed. They are barometers of what and who we and our informants are or have been at the precise time of writing and in the past.

Crucially, we have embarked on this project from the standpoint of being fathers and sons of fathers, and of researching in a narrative sense the experiences of others who have been so. The interactionsist approach we adopt is essential, as the lives and destinies of fathers and sons are intertwined. At various points we provide personal interrogation of the aspects of fatherhood that have caused us joy, anxiety, challenges, self-doubt, pain and professional curiosity. The issues which this orientation prompts cover much of the negative landscape which is the habitual territory of a significant minority of fathers and their sons. Thus we tackle a wide range of issues which are at various levels problematic and which present personal or social challenges.

We explore some aspects of masculinity and the roles that are played out in the father/son relationship, beginning with the recently developed emphasis on male role-modelling in the early years of child-rearing. We also draw on the fathers' experiences of schooling, and consider how this affects their subsequent contact with educational institutions, and in particular its long-term impact on the expectations and performances of their sons. We have both struggled with at times being absent and unsatisfactory fathers. This, together with the impact of bereavement – again personally experienced both as fathers and as sons – is the focus of chapters in the book. And we attempt some scoping of what it is to be a father in a complex contemporary world, where gender roles are increasingly debated and blurred and where male involvement in a variety of erstwhile female-dominated aspects of their son's education is subject to ever increasing scrutiny and question.

A father's view of this complex role-ecosystem is captured by Tony Soprano (as Dads we sit on sofas and watch the television) in his macho-posture as a soap-opera Mafia godfather: 'It's your problem. For you to deal with'. Chin-up, head down. Don't say a word, don't shed a tear. The pervasive, patriarchal culture of just making do. The reader will find these sentiments woven through this volume.

As we write we are cast adrift amidst a sea of myth, half-truth and studied oversight. Fathers and their own fathers? Fathers and their sons? And the stories of their sons? The good, the bad and the ugly uneasily residing close to home, and sometimes in our own homes. Of course, the good should be celebrated. Fathers are integral to the existence of their sons, and well before the public testosterone-fuelled celebration of a birth ('I've proved that I'm a man') it is recognised that most fathers find huge emotional fulfilment at the birth of their child (McKeown, 2001). This is another part of our personal and professional experience and should be borne in mind as an antidote to some of the negative themes that have drawn us, moth-like, to their light. We both recall that when we were early career professionals over 25 years ago, Jackson (1984) was reminding us how the existing academic literature was mainly about 'abnormal' fathers: the ordinary, everyday dad seemed to be invisible in this literature, the silent majority who stand aside in the face of others' misfortunes. We are, therefore, providing a counterbalance, with the often marginal fatherings we give account of here: we have grown and learned immeasurably as fathers, and it has brought inexpressible joy.

Although our choice of themes is broad-ranging each chapter in *Fathers and Sons* is organised in a similar way. Each opens with narrative accounts that are drawn from personalised recollections or inventions and from a range of father and son situations and relationships. These are bare-knuckle data, for the purist may not like what they see, may feel affronted by their nakedness and wish to retreat to the more established comfort-zones of educational enquiry.

We have categorised these data in three narrative sets which illustrate the father and son diaspora: fathers as adult sons, talking retrospectively about their own fathers during childhood and adolescence (identified in the text by the suffix 'A'); fathers commenting on being a father, in relation to their child or adolescent son (identified by the letter 'B'); and sons themselves providing insights into their own experiences of childhood and adolescence in relation to their father (identified by the letter 'C'). The letters identify these narrative perspectives throughout the book.

As we have indicated and periodically reinforce, the narrative extracts are snapshots taken randomly from a variety of sources and by various means. Typically, they have been elicited by recalling personal experiences, by drawing on conversation with close friends or acquaintances, and by obtaining accounts from fathers and sons with whom we have come in contact at various stages during our work. The data from each source have been obtained in free conversation and largely unstructured interviews. In each case our fathers and sons were audio-recorded, according to the conventions of current ethical procedures (BERA, 2004). A few respondents preferred to convey their thoughts in writing. And a small group of trusted colleagues – teachers, teacher-educators, fathers – formed an informal reference group, whose advice and input was occasionally sought.

Our methodology draws upon narratives from informants we encountered personally and professionally. We have used their words to serve the reader with data which provides a multi-textured account of the histories, contemporary lives and futures of our exemplar fathers and sons. Ultimately amidst our literature overviews and practical considerations, they remind us that our fathers and sons are real people. These are not data used to promote a methodological dogma or position: they are real words with real meanings for real people. And although we have taken meanings from these words as they have been spoken or written at the end of each narrative section, these are stories which stand alone in their telling, and from which those working in education, and other fathers and their sons, can draw.

The second part of each chapter presents discussion about some of the theoretical and conceptual matters which seem to be embedded in the data. Again, we are led by our own histories and interests as fathers and sons. This is the stuff of real-world research, with its attendant real-world frailties, uncertainties and challenges. Each chapter continues with observations on the implications for those working for, with and as fathers, and the various ways they interface with sons and with a society which, as we discuss, holds pathologised views of a man's role in education. The data we work with in this book is in many respects left red-raw and sometimes stinging. Our commitment to certain core fathering principles then leads us to present our suggestions for practitioners. These are practical initiatives we have heard about, participated in and which may be of widespread value in educational settings.

Thus, the final sections of each chapter together make up a set of suggestions for professionals working in schools and for fathers and their sons, gathered from a variety of sources. Some are strategies and ways of working we have encountered during our work with teachers and teaching assistants. Others are drawn from the principal informants whose data provides many of the narrative extracts which illustrate each chapter. And others are the result of our own lived experience of being fathers.

Finally, it is important that these 'recommendations' should be viewed in a context in which, partly as a result of a vibrant, if complex, agenda relating to *Every Child Matters* (2001), the vast majority of schools are aware of the need to provide consistent and ongoing support to fathers experiencing challenges in the parenting of their boys. Accordingly, our suggestions should be read not as admonitions but as reminders. And they should be viewed not so much as work in progress but rather as starting points, highlighting the infancy of overt father-and-son focused practices some educational settings. As well as a bibliography, we list useful electronic resources providing information, discussion forums and other forms of support for fathers and sons.

2

Land of my fathers and sons: an overview

He was there as I left, proud and smiling at the caged window at once bright and slowly going away. I never said goodbye. The hospital was grey. No! Grey was not the colour. It was black and white, a photograph etched on and in my mind – a memory which I will never escape – the greyness of that landscape. It was the same memory of my allotment-cling to his trouser-leg whilst trying to be a man beyond my years; the photograph there to record his warmth and dignity as a Dad, and my mantelpiece still now is heavy with that emotion. I'd played with this man and cried with him too; been made fearful of his anger and stillness at times; I'd shared all those things a son is supposed to share and some things more than that. I never said goodbye. To this day I still wonder why that was. It has become part of my quest for understanding, but informed by a fear that he may have been wondering why this was exactly so. Why had I, his son, never said goodbye? I now escape, creeping from the household in these days of lightness and summer, wondering if they'll say 'He never said goodbye'. Living, you could say, those moments of regret over my last eternities.

And they do of course. My life is now filled to bursting with demands that I juggle, precariously and never in the accomplished manner of the circus performer, plate-spinning. Dexterous skills of the mind, some psychological toughness. That's what I needed then and I certainly need it now. It's the blind terror of goings away – whether me or my children, but especially my big boy, who now strides over my consciousness and brings meaning to my metaphor of never saying that goodbye. He's Daniel and Dad, rolled into one.

As I write this down, fitfully and with unbearable blandness – brutalising the reader without thought or decency – I struggle to make sense of these jangly-guitar emotional strings for who I am, who my own children, my own boy will become no doubt in time. Such is the indelible print of the psychological consciousness. Nor does it really connect with me that this book, this enterprise, this work of exemplary crudeness has ceased – has long since ceased – to be the work that it set out to be. Woven between the words you read, the cue-phrases which summon up a down-view of who men are when they become fathers, is the wilful intent of at least one author who needs to find meanings for who he is. And who are we, then? These 'fathers' and 'sons'? [A]

Being me, the son ... well interesting 'cos I'm seeing my life in front of me, all there. That's going to be me. He's my Dad ... I like ... I think he's OK, my Dad, and I think he's been good to us, me and my sister. I want to be like him, but then I feel very bad and think that's not what he'd like ... because Dads always want something better for their kids, and boys mainly ... they want to be able to feel that they've done a good job in being a Dad. And it'll be me I'd say. I'll be just like him, wanting my kids ... well all of them yes, all of these ... boys and girls, but the boys, to be much better than ... not better in that way but, to do well and get more out of it than me. I think that's natural. That's the life that Dad's have... [A]

It comes and goes ... the feeling you know ... when you want to ... I don't know how ... well, the feeling ... it's you know, that I'm responsible for these kids, they're my lads and sometimes it's like, well, I'm so full of being worried 'cos I'm not as good as other Dads. You know? They don't say it and I'd say they don't think like that at all you know. But it's like, as they're getting older, they're getting more like me. Well, not like me, ugly bastard and that ... like me in the things they do, you know. Most blokes if they were true to themselves would say that, I'd say [B]

Magic, all the time mate. I so love it, being a Dad and doing all this stuff with him. It's my chance to play again, with all the things I never had first time around. It's great, really good ... and, funny, I see the funny side of it too, when there's a bit of mucking about, mischief and all that ... You shouldn't, but inside myself, in here ... I'm really smiling to myself because

... well ... that's me, me as a kid myself ... all over again. That sort of thing, when you realise it's happening, it's magic [B]

Dad's cool mainly. Good ... he sometimes gets in a bit of a nark, and you can tell, but most of the time it's good, really good. He's not got a lot of friends, other Dads or stuff ... like that ... but I'm his big mate I think and we're good together we get on good ... I like it when I'm with him, it's neat doing things with him [C]

We never talk about him no more. He's history, nothing ... He was bad to everybody, really bad ... if he came in through there I'd punch him, punch his fucking lights out. Most of all it makes me ... get angry, hot inside when I think of what he did ... I was alright, me, I was not in the way. It was Ryan (older brother) who caught it first ... he stood up to him, that bit older you know but still he was, well..12 or maybe 13 then, and not really old at all really. He would come up and be crying and shouting and he'd been belted or slapped or something for nothing ... no nothing at all, other than that he was there, just in the way ... But that wasn't the baddest thing. It was the worst, fuck it was bad when he started on Mum, and you could hear it happen, you know ... that was bad, very, very bad. It was the worst because all you could do was hear it from upstairs and it was ... I think it was like being in a film or something, it can't happen, doesn't happen like this. But it was, and I was fucking 7 or something and my Mum was being kicked all round the fucking kitchen by that bastard. Too right, I'd fucking knife him if I saw him [C]

Themes highlighted by these fathers and sons in their narratives:

- insecurity in a changing social system
- the importance of relationships
- the responsibility of being a dad
- re-visiting childhoods
- subliminal or overt 'competition' with other dads
- broken or abusive relationships

We too have been sons of fathers and we are both fathers of sons. This constitutes the rationale for this book. But we are firm in our contention that there are important psycho-social issues at work in 'being male' in the 21st century, and that these are played out against a backdrop of economic globalisation and demographic change. Put simply, the old sureties of being male, the 'head' of a household, a 'father-figure': these notions of patriarchy have been slowly but perceptibly diminishing throughout the last few decades.

The study of fathers, fatherhood and their sons is not a recent phenomenon. Although this book adopts a particular focus – fathers and sons and their involvement in education – it is helpful to recognise this historical context. It informs the themes we have identified and allows recognition of the long-standing complexities inherent in being a father and a son. It also provides something of a justification for this book, beyond the personal drivers highlighted in our introduction. A survey of the less recent literature on fathers confirms that there is little which places an explicit focus on fathers and their sons. In consequence, our historical summary of the broad-brush themes which inform the topic have to draw principally from published sources which deal with men in the generic role-context of parenting.

The social and economic position of men in the modern period – the eighteenth, nineteenth and twentieth centuries – dramatically changed as a result of widespread shifts in the way families functioned. Prior to the mid-eighteenth century the father was at the centre of a patriarchal and extended family unit. The family was at the centre of 'community' and within it the man's role as patriarch was unquestioned. The family functioned as the place of education, as well as it being the 'church', 'hospital', 'old people's home' and 'court' (Hareven, 1971). The onset of the modern age, however, saw the functions of the family being reduced as more and more services were adopted by the emergent structures of newly industrialised countries. This was accompanied by a decline in the authority and responsibility of the father (Bloom-Feshbach, 1981). Already, therefore, we can identify the important theme of role-change and a subsequent search for meaning and identity which has continued into the post-modern era.

The advent of industrialisation brought with it the move of the father away from the family home for longer periods, affecting the status of the father within the family unit: 'Working away from home, the father was an intermittent boss and authority model at best' (Stearns, 1979). This diminution of status was accompanied by a large-scale shift from an agrarian, land-based economy to a dependence on industrial production which enabled both women and sons to enter the labour market. In consequence the authority of the father was perceptibly diminished. Stearns (*op.cit.*) illustrates this when he comments 'A survey of literary autobiographies (from about 1750 to 1900) traces growing hostility to fathers ... Too many fathers were asserting authority that they no longer really possessed'. So a further historical theme, revisited at several points in this book, can be added: the conflict between the provider function of the father and his consequent absence from the home, with its impact on his personal relationship with his son.

A further important effect of industrialisation, increasingly felt throughout the nineteenth and into the twentieth centuries, was the change in the ways in which men interacted with others. Pleck (1979) summarises this development, arguing that, in the pre-modern period, men moved from an interpersonal style in which such things as tenderness and vulnerability were viewed as uncharacteristic. Rather, men were expected to exhibit compulsive behaviour and to act out aggression and anger, especially with other males, as a manifestation of their masculinity. The modern age brought a re-assessment of this situation: emotional expression and heterosexual intimacy was encouraged, whilst the ability to remain emotionally cool rather than impulsive came to be regarded as a major attribute. And it seems to us to be the case that contemporary fathers and their sons sometimes evidence a continuation of the struggle to find an effective psychological response between 'traditional' and 'modern' masculinities. Evidence of their struggle surfaces regularly in this book.

A final theme we have identified is that growth-orientated capitalist economies in the modern and post-modern age, with their emphasis upon upward mobility through competition, material acquisitiveness and status amongst peers has resulted dramatic changes in the way families function. Bronfenbrenner (1975) has remarked on these trends, stating that they are damaging to the quality of the lives of children. The quest to 'achieve', as measured by socially recognised indicators such as job, house, car, holidays and so on, places a dramatic burden on families as a whole, and upon those men who are rooted, often out of necessity, in a 'provider' model of fatherhood.

The psychological effects of these demands placed on fathers serve to compound the negative effect of his physical absence from the home, already noted as one product of industrialisation, and now a feature of contemporary socio-economic functioning. In the modern and post-modern age the father is also psychologically removed from the family. Some commentators relate this to the increasing abstractness of modern employment compared to the overtly concrete jobs that men held previously. And whereas before industrialisation fathers were the major influence on their son's socialisation, that role has now diminished as a result of factors such as electronic communication: first radio and television and now mobile telephones and personal computers. And in terms of the sons themselves, there have been long-standing concerns that the legitimate absence of fathers on account of the need to provide financially for the family, results in long term damage to sons. Freud (1923) stressed the need for sons to rebel against a father's authority, as a natural part of their development. If the father is psychologically as well as physically absent, their normal development is interrupted.

Recognition of these broad contexts enables us to understand the nature of what some have described as the 'pain and confusion' amongst males – both fathers and sons (Jolliff and Horne, 1999) – a situation which is exacerbated in post-industrialised nations by global changes. And it is also important in aiding an understanding of the role of fathers and sons in the 'cycles of disadvantage' which have characterised much theorising on marginalised or excluded populations in the last thirty or so years (Rutter and Madge, 1976; Welshman, 2006). So there is considerable evidence to suggest that difficulties experienced by fathers, including those relating to socialisation, family relationships, learning and citizenship, are influenced by a number of environmental continuities. Quinton and Rutter (1988) suggest that 'parenting breakdown' is characterised by such things as institutionalised rearing as a child, marital breakdown, an un-supportive, deviant or absent spouse, resorting to marriage 'to escape', marrying under pressure from parents, and poor social functioning as adult.

In viewing these features of parenting breakdown one should be cautious about affirming causal relationships unilaterally. We would entirely follow the interpretations of Rutter (1997) in arguing that whilst there is an intergenerational link between, for example, 'deviant' fathers and 'deviant' sons, we must stop well short of claiming genetic transference. Equally, too, it is necessary to recognise that many 'at-risk' fathers and 'at-risk' sons do remain resilient to the negative factors associated with parenting breakdown and its consequences. And so, whilst we do focus on a particularised and partial set of fathering experiences, which lean towards the problematic, the fractured and the tentative, and which arrive prompted by an admix of our own personal and professional life experiences, we similarly acknowledge that many fathers are more resilient, engaged and continuously optimistic than some of those portrayed in this book.

Recent policy orientations in England, most notably by New Labour from 1997 onwards, have sought to address two major issues in education: pupil behaviour and achievement and their emotional health and well-being (DfEE, 1998). In each case there is a consistent, often complex, set of linkages to the lives and careers of fathers and sons. Boys are heavily over-represented in the numbers of pupils attending special schools for pupils experiencing social, emotional and behavioural difficulties (SEBD) (DfES, 2006). Boys also comprise by far the majority of pupils excluded from schools or presenting problematic, challenging or disruptive behaviours within them. These statistics run alongside lower levels of achievement in key national curriculum subjects.

In the case of exclusion, Wright, Weekes and McGlaughlin (2000) have articulated the growing evidence of the overrepresentation of boys, especially by those from particular racial, cultural or socio-economic groups. The Audit Commission (1999) also notes the prevalence of boys in exclusion figures, whilst Skidmore (2007) reveals further alarming facts concerning exclusions in England in general. He shows that 72 per cent of all fixed-term exclusions and 79 per cent of permanent exclusions comprised boys. Furthermore, 54 per cent of all fixed-term exclusions and 51 per cent of permanent exclusions were boys aged 12-14 years. Finally, and perhaps most dramatically, Skidmore states that one in five of all boys aged 13 have been subject to a fixed-term exclusion during Year 8 or 9 of their secondary schooling. Leaving aside the clearly stated political bias of this research, with its right-of-centre orientation, the depressing overall thesis is echoed in other national performance figures for boys in schools (DCSF, 2007).

In England there has been significant growth in recent years in the educational underachievement of boys (Frater, 1997; DfES/DoH, 2003) and their apparent lack of motivation (NFER, 1995; Shipman and Hicks, 2001). They are over-represented amongst pupils who under-perform academically (Ofsted, 2001). And they form the highest proportion of pupils whose SEN is related to moderate learning difficulties (NfER, 2004). Central to responses to this major national concern in education has been a focus on the involvement of parents: policy guidance from central government, for example, exhorts schools to 'Try to encourage males at home to be actively involved in pupils' homework' and a warning not to 'assume that support is being provided to boys from male role models in the home' (DfES/DoH, *op. cit*).

Boys become men. Men comprise the large majority of the prison population in England – in 2003 there were over 69,000 male inmates, compared to about 4,500 female inmates (Home Office, 2003). They are far more likely to be implicated in violent or aggressive behaviour (Hines and Saudino, 2006) and substance or alcohol abuse. Hobcraft (1998), using data from the National Child Development Study, poignantly illustrates the careers, roots and destinies of boys into men. He shows that parental interest in schooling is in a cluster of factors most likely to determine the subsequent social and economic inclusion of young people moving into adulthood. He states that boys with step-parents are nearly three times more likely to be homeless between the ages of 23 and 33; such boys were over four times less likely to gain degree-equivalent qualifications.

Hobcraft (1998) goes on to highlight a 'massive and progressive' association between boys' low educational test scores and a doubling in adult risk of such inclusion (or exclusion) indicators as early parenthood, 'adult malaise', living in social housing, receipt of benefits and not receiving high income. His summary of this ongoing feature of English society, based on the evidence currently available, was that 'Fathers' lack of interest in schooling is a particularly powerful and progressive predictor of lack of qualifications, with persistent low interest ... quadrupling the risk ... '. Such 'risk', is bluntly, failure to thrive economically, being socially excluded from communities on account of mental health or other lifestyle issues, and having a significant tendency to engage in crime or other anti-social activity.

Fathers and sons are strongly implicated in criminal careers. Historical and contemporary evidence shows that boys from families in which the father has engaged or continues to engage in criminal activity are more likely to become involved in delinquency and adult crime themselves (Farrington and Jolliffe, 2005). The routines and life-style of young or adolescent boys are strong predictors of offending. Adolescents who spend much of their time with their peers and little with their family also tend to be more involved in offending than others (ESRC, 2006). Boys are more likely than girls to report having negative contact with the police for the first time at age 12 or under (ESYTC, 2003). There is also long-standing research evidence which draws our attention to the likelihood of male offenders to be involved in violent crime and in the continuities between aggression or 'problem' behaviour amongst boys and subsequent adult violence (Home Office, 1991; Farrington, 1995).

At this stage in the reading, fathers can be forgiven for assuming that we are adopting an uncritical and pathologising overview. To an extent we are, in that the focus of this book is to strip back some of the tensions and frailties that are inherent in the interface between masculinity, fatherhood and society. We are by no means briefing on 'fatherhood' as a generality, and accept that for a substantial proportion of fathers and their sons there is a relationship of fulfilment, joy, familial love and belonging and an optimistic view of the future. Such relationships, as research consistently demonstrates, are a major contributor to building resilience to the negative delineations of 'being male' and its manifestation in father-son relationships. But – and we pose this subliminal question throughout the book – what happens when the equilibrium is fractured, when fathers no longer connect with sons, or do so in ways that are hostile, inhumane or in ways which celebrate or otherwise project lifestyle images that articulate the anti-social, the exclusionary or, still worse, the delinquent or the criminal? Or when fathers and sons encounter life-pressures and challenges to which they respond or endeavour to manage in ways which are unsatisfactorily rooted in a traditional masculine idiom?

It is these tenuous, discontinuous and at times negative eventualities that this book highlights, illustrated by the observations and commentaries by fathers and sons. These highlight the stark contrasts between actualised and connected fathering and their positive effect on relationships, achievement and social belonging. And the issues they raise for the extended, re-modelled and hopefully newly empowered professional workforce in schools, should be fundamental to the new education agenda of the 21st century.

Some considerations for practitioners

Vital amongst the various challenges posed by *The Children's Plan* (DCSF, 2007) is a need to acquire new insights into the participation of fathers in the education of their sons. Such insights need to be sketched around a set of knowledge which enables greater levels of understanding about the ways in which fathers influence the educational and social behaviour of their sons. This influence is in part located in a self-fulfilling tradition that mothers do education and care, and that fathers act as mainly passive contributors. They are available mainly in times of crisis – whether as a disciplinarian ('*Just wait until your Dad sees this ... he'll be so annoyed that you don't work more carefully*' [B]), as a decision-make regarding non-standard school activity ('*My Mum said she'd ask my Dad, see what he thinks, and if he says so then I can go ... I've got my fingers crossed, all my friends are going*' [C]), or as a complainant ('*So I said to the wife, leave 'em to me, and I gave 'em a piece of my mind ... that's the only way you'll get any sense out of them ...*' [B]).

These ways of interacting with their sons and with schools is located in fathers' masculine-type response to pressure or adversity. And this functions alongside their position within shifting social order, in which the old order comprising a sequential journey from boys' games, male-orientated schooling (woodwork, motor vehicle studies, technical drawing and so on), to apprenticeship to a 'trade', again dominated by masculine rites of passage, to finally become a male-breadwinner, a role that has long been in decline. It has the potential to leave both men and boys in an unforgiving and unsupported frontier zone made up of new emotional, social and economic territories. Education systems as a whole, and schools and individual workers need to consider how they respond to this challenge. Their respective choices will determine whether they are part of the problem or part of the solution.

One necessity will be to develop a systematic and planned approach to assembling a training portfolio which will enable participants to assimilate new professional orientations towards fathers and sons. These must out of necessity enshrine coverage of child development in relation to gender differences, the psychology of male parenting, the sociology of fatherhood and masculinity in a changing world, and consideration of the ways in which new knowledge about boys and their fathers might have practice-related implications for schools and other settings.

In conclusion, such a dynamic approach to progressing a male agenda in schools seems to be essential at policy level. These are enshrined within *The Children's Plan* (2007) and echo many of the concerns identified regarding the marginalisation of men and boys in 21st century post-industrialised education systems. Thus, the Plan will seek to 'involve parents fully in their child's learning' (p3) by recognising that 'we need particularly to improve how government and services involve fathers' in order to 'help every parent do the best for their child' (p8). So the current government is setting in place plans to 'encourage and support fathers so that they can play a bigger role in their children's lives, both at home and in school. Some fathers bring up children on their own, and we will ensure that services are responsive to the particular issues they face' (p19). One practical exemplar of work in this area, provided within *The Children's Plan* outlines the following interventions (see page 20).

These policy imperatives are concrete manifestations that the role of fathers in education needs to be a focal point for ground level action. In making such an overt statement, and setting aside a tendency to regard such announcements as pious intent, *The Children's Plan* is perhaps the first time that fathers and their sons have become the dedicated focus of national action. This represents genuine progress.

Box 1.1: Engaging fathers

'*My dad has helped me the most; in Year 7 I had loads of trouble and I didn't want to go into school, but he encouraged me and supported me loads.*' (Young girl, Liverpool)

We know that children benefit enormously from having strong relationships with their fathers, yet public services routinely fail to engage with fathers, particularly when the father does not live with the child. We will work with the Children's Workforce Development Council and the new National Academy for Parenting Practitioners to ensure that occupational standards and training for the workforce will reflect the need for public services to engage with both father and mother except where there is a clear risk to the child to do so.

As we move towards offering more regular up-to-date information on a child's progress (set out in Chapter 3) we will expect schools to keep contact details of all parents living apart from their children, to involve them where possible, and to identify and use best practice in engaging fathers.

In developing Parent Know-How we are taking account of ways in which information can be made more easily accessible for fathers, mindful of research which shows that 63 per cent of fathers say that their preferred channel for information and support is the internet.

As we increase outreach through Sure Start Children's Centres we will look to engage fathers, offering them support in strengthening their parenting skills.

Department of Children Schools and Families (2007) *The Children's Plan.* London: DCSF, p25

3

The literature on fathers and sons

I look up to him, even though he's not here. I think I look up to him a lot. Not as a God or anything, but as somebody who has taught me about being a father myself and about loyalty, about always trying to do the right thing, always being there even if its hard or inconvenient. I think I am doing this a lot more as I get older too, thinking along the lines of 'What would Dad have done now?' or whenever I'm thinking of getting out of doing something, a job round the house or whatever you can think of, I'll hear myself saying 'Dad wouldn't have done that' and I'd then think that he'd be very disappointed if he knew that I was letting him down. And I reckon that'd be right too [A]

There are some things that I'd rather not say about me and my Dad. Nothing ... nasty, or anything, just ... well, things about him, his personality, the things he sometimes ... no, that's not it ... it's the way he sometimes comes across, you know? As a son I think, that's not really very good, not nice at all and I want to push that away. I know its part of him, being distant and unfriendly some of the time, and there's a good side to him, but I don't want it to be like that with my own lad, no way [A]

He's an irritating little shit, to be honest and sometimes I'd be that far, just that, far from wringing the little bastard's neck. He winds me up something rotten he does. I mean, he gets everything. It's not as though he's not looked after. Me and Michelle work hard to provide for all three of them but sometimes ... well, Robbie is the worst, the others aren't bad actually. With Robbie it's all about him, all about Robbie. Did we do it? Did we make him like that? Or is it just down to me, him being a lad and that? Or maybe it's the age thing, growing up and wanting to be that bit older [B]

I always go up to give them a kiss goodnight, always ... without fail. I don't know what it is, and it might seem terrible ... but I always reserve a special ... maybe a bit of ... just an extra bit of contact, or a touch ... for him, because he is the first one, you know, the first born, the lad who'll one day be me I suppose [B]

Its best at the weekends, it's definitely best then. He takes me football training first, cos Mum's got the little ones and they can't really do that. He never sits in his car or goes off and leaves me, he watches, even when it's really raining and I like that, I think it's really good because there's not too many of the others whose Dad does it. We go to the match straight away usually after I've done the training. Yeah, it's a good time, because we can talk, really catch up with all sorts but honestly, I think its mainly, mostly ... about football and stuff, unless there's been something that we've needed to sort out [C]

I don't see him all that much, not as much as my Mum. He's always out doing things. Always at work or down the pub with his mates. I see him mostly at the weekends and sometimes he'll say, let's go here or there and stuff. But then, I think he does it mainly because he wants to go, you know? [C]

Themes highlighted by these fathers and sons in their narratives:

- father's need to understand child/adolescent development
- fathers as role models
- the recognition of a need for closeness
- sons strive for companionship from their dads
- special relationships with a specific son

Theoretical and conceptual issues relating to being fathers and sons in education systems, and articulated as such in academic and professional writing, are relatively rare in generic education literature – although it is important to point out that there is a correspondingly substantial, and historically more abundant, output in scholarship and research in sociology, social policy, health, youth and adolescence studies and so on (see, for example, Fein, 1978; Feldman, Nash and Aschenbrenner, 1983; Marsiglio, Day and Lamb, 2000). In studies which have education as a focus, the emphasis has been upon parents and to a lesser extent families. Materials which account for policy and practice in respect of 'parents' and schools have proliferated (Vincent, 2000; Crozier and Reay, 2005) but they make almost no specific reference to fathers. Such a situation seems odd, given that we nowadays assume a more focused gaze on issues of gender and equality. And even within that multitude of materials on the practicalities of promoting parents as participants in the education system, relatively little has been made of the discrete role played by fathers in relation their sons – although recent policy initiatives in several countries (for example, England, Australia and USA) illustrate increasing attention to the father's role.

Both being a child and raising children are landmark events and periods in the lives of most adults. For men, who will *de facto* have themselves been sons, fatherhood is viewed as 'life's fullest expression of masculinity' (Pittman, 2006). Yet notions of fatherhood have been changing over many generations. The Industrial Revolution, for instance, has defined much of what came to be viewed as the functional position of fathers within families and, by extension, their relationship with their sons. Moves away from land-based economies to those of industrialised production in the late 18th century meant that families needed to have someone who would regularly go out from the home to work to support the family. For the succeeding 200 or so years, that person has in most cases been the man. Setting aside psycho-social and biological reasons, one rationale was the straightforward fact that men couldn't produce milk for food – and, historically, bottle-feeding was not an option. So masculinity – including the process of being a father – ceased to be substantially delineated by involvement in domestic activity and therefore the process of child-rearing. Thus, girls usually received gendered benefits from their childhoods but boys did not.

In post-industrialised nations, the modern era is characterised by fathers occupying a position of power and privilege outside the home and family, as an employer or employee. As breadwinner, the father came to be the principal provider of material resources, food, clothing and shelter. But alongside this came an increasing tendency to perceive the male position as both marginal to the 'real' goal and business of the home: the rearing of offspring, and to all that this complex activity enshrined. Fathers became less integrally involved in play and other developmental interactions with their children, less involved in decisions about, and the processes of, the schooling of their offspring, and less connected with social interchanges involving adults but centered around children because of absence forced by the requirements of work.

An interesting and relatively recent development – certainly apparent since after the Second World War – has been the gradual shift in employment patterns, part of which at least has acted as a counterbalance to the gendering of the home and one of its principal functions. Central to this shift are two features. First, the increase in the number of working mothers, and the small and less important phenomenon of the so-called house-husband, has given mothers and fathers an opportunity to take more equable roles in child-rearing, although this itself has not necessarily influenced father-son relationships. This could be the subject of useful research: homes are now much busier places which are frequently more an extension of the workplace than an insulation from it. It could be argued that fathers have even less opportunity to interact with their children and that the conditions of what social intercourse does exist have been subject to gradual deterioration in terms of quality. Evidence suggests that these socio-economic changes have become more pronounced and the rate of changes in fatherhood patterns has accelerated (Lewis and Lamb, 2007).

It is this later period of rapid change both in fathering and being a son that we explore, in sketching a brief literature. We wish to articulate some of the recent and current themes we consider to be central to the educational dimension of fathers and sons. So, again, we are opting for the particular, providing what is a selective scoping of this important territory.

First we need to establish a personal position. In much the same way that our orientation to being fathers and sons ourselves informs and influences our choice of focal points for this book, we are similarly partisan when we survey the recent literature. In each of our various approaches to fathering and being a son we are making claims for the development and practice of 'living theories' (Whitehead, 2004) – although we are conscious that our efforts to do this are mundane and one-dimensional compared to the rich literature that now exists concerning this orientation.

As 'living theorists' we inhabit territory which is personal, becomes ever more personal, and is not measurable or evaluated by pre-existing templates, protocols or ordinances. Certainly, it is unlikely that we'd be comfortable about having our data shoe-horned into a predetermined interpretative tradition. But the complex process of being a father, and that of being a son, is paralleled by the disparate though interconnected approaches that have sought to illuminate and interrogate it (Day *et al*, 2005). Whilst recognising the existence of this approach to mapping the research orientations of studies of fathers, we retain connection, as researchers and scholars, with the personal process of living fatherhood in its various forms.

Something also needs to be said at the outset about masculinity, fatherhood and sons. This is important for, as Harris (1994) pointedly remarked in the context of sons 'trying to become men' in contemporary settings where the impact of societal changes are most keenly felt, 'We need to re-learn what masculinity really is'. 'Masculinity' in relation to boys and to the sons they always are and the fathers they will most likely become, is a contemporary problematic. For example, Jolliff and Horne (1999) draw attention both to the 'tragic consequences of fatherlessness in America today' and to a corresponding increase in the range and frequency of boys' interactions with women. Boys 'without fathers', for example, are hugely over-represented amongst those who exhibit violent misbehaviour in school (Sheline, Skipper and Broadhead, 1994), where they are statistically far more likely to encounter teachers and other professionals who are female (Jolliff and Horne, 1999). A similar situation prevails in England and other parts of Europe. In terms of education, boys and adolescent males comprise the group which are more likely to:

- have school attendance problems
- experience learning difficulties
- present 'disruptive' acting-out behaviour
- under-achieve academically
- attend special schools or settings
- leave school early

The poignancy of this over-representation of boys is amplified when viewed in relation to the characteristics of adult males. Ackerman (1993) has used the expression 'silent sons' to depict adults who display an inability to sustain relationships, an inability to control anger, an addictive personality and a strong likelihood of low self-esteem. A further characteristic identified by Ackerman is emotional introversion; the silent son keeps himself to himself and has a significant fear of criticism.

Furthermore, silent sons experience a condition referred to as co-dependency, a product of prolonged exposure to environments and cultures which inhibit open discussion of feelings or of personal concerns. The co-dependent man feels unable to display emotion and often relies on women to act out their emotional side, whilst also tending to live their lives through the lives of their sons. The personality picture of an emotionally isolated individual is completed by a fear of intimacy and an overstated masculinity.

These issues are germane to the careers and eventual destinies of both fathers and sons today. Pleck and Masciadrelli (2004) indicate that, during the last two decades, there has been a demonstrable 'culture shift' towards greater male domesticity in the UK. Meanwhile Fisher, McCulloch and Gershuny (1999) have shown that the childcare responsibilities of British fathers have increased far more since the 1960s than those of mothers. With such involvement comes role confusion, changed expectations and tensions: Lewis (2000), for example, highlighted an increase in marital dissatisfaction where dual-earners were both involved in childcare – with potential implications for the well-being of their children.

Research studies directed towards cohabiting partners have increased in the last decade, in part prompted by the social change which has caused a dramatic shift in the way 'families' are constructed and operate (ONS, 2003). Cohabiting relationships have been shown to be more likely to dissolve. Smart and Stevens (2000) highlight a continuum of commitment by partners in cohabiting relationships, ranging from full engagement to an acceptance that the relationship was unlikely to last. Even more pertinently, Speak, Cameron and Gilroy (1997) refer to the emergent tensions between work and home amongst young unwed fathers, so that they tend to fail to meet their parental responsibilities. Reference has been made to 'dangerous fathers': those who usually live in poverty and are incapable of sustaining positive relationships with their children.

On the other hand, notwithstanding the increases in fathers' involvement in child-rearing, a body of research evidence suggests that it is a mother's relationship that is most influential in the sociability of primary-age children (Steele *et al*, 1999). Whilst this may be understandable, given the identity crisis that the social changes referred to have created, it may nevertheless further exacerbate the difficulties faced by fathers in coming to terms with their masculinity, in that both overtly and subliminally – and in spite of reorientating the role of 'father' – it is the mother who retains familial primacy.

Recent research has also identified an increasingly complex array of types of fathering. Lee (2005), for instance, has identified 73 different patterns of fatherhood in her sample, and notes that more than a third of the current generation of male parents have followed what she calls a 'non-standard paternal biography'. And it is likely that even 'traditional' fathering is now far more complex and uncertain.

The Labour government's commitment to supporting the role of fathers in education has been a core dimension of their social policy; certainly, the change in emphasis from the generic and context-neutral 'education' (as in Department for Education and Skills) to 'family' (as in Department for Children Schools and Families) communicates an understanding that education is as much a dimension of families as it is of schools. Several important studies on the role of fathers in family groupings have emerged during this period. Welsh *et al* (2004) explored fathers' involvement in rearing secondary-age children and noted that when there was conflict between parents, children were more likely to experience emotional and behavioural difficulties. Interviews carried out for the study highlighted the persistence of a traditional view of fathering, in which the man's role was to 'be there' and to provide for the physical needs of his children. These researchers also found that many fathers claimed that fathering 'came naturally', but they admitted that they often lacked the confidence to establish or maintain close relationships with their children (Welsh *et al*, 2004).

Mental health issues have been a major policy consideration for the government during the last ten years, and these have particularly sought to address the emotional needs of children, for example via initiatives such as the 'social and emotional competence' programme (Weare and Gray, 2003). Recent research published in medical journals has brought home the importance of this topic: Ramchandani *et al* (2005) suggest that there are discernable links between post-natal depression in fathers and subsequent emotional and behavioural issues in their sons. They found that where fathers had been suffering from depression soon after the birth, their children were twice as likely to have severe emotional and behavioural problems. They reported that boys in their sample were more affected than girls. They state that 'the influence of fathers in very early childhood may have been underestimated in the past ... but these findings indicate that paternal depression has a specific and persisting negative impact on children's early behavioural and emotional development'.

Recently research efforts have been directed towards young fathers, a group which had not attracted substantial attention from policy makers before (Ferguson and Hogan, 2004). Young fathers tend to be characterised by low academic attainment and show a correlation with anti-social behaviour (Bunting and McAuley, 2004). Moreover, such fathers often experience conditions of economic and social disadvantage: many will have been in Local Authority care and have experienced violence or sexual abuse at home. Very few will have had models of good fathering (*Young Voice*, 2005). And it will come as little surprise that research on the life trajectories of such fathers reveals them to be at high risk of engaging in crime or abusive behaviour towards women and of experiencing negative emotions like fear, anxiety and anger (Jaffee *et al*, 2001).

Father-and-son relationships directly in (rather than about) education have seen an increased emphasis over the last twenty or so years, in part because of the attention directed by schools to the establishment of stronger home-school links. Research is unequivocal in finding that positive outcomes follow when fathers are directly involved in their son's education. Thus, for example, Lloyd (1999) interviewed 52 boys and 22 fathers and reported that most of the fathers said that their son's reading was their responsibility and that their involvement had enhanced their son's level of literacy. Fisher, McCulloch and Gershuny (1999) also highlight the educational gains made by children as a result of fathers' involvement. The international literature on fathers and their involvement in education is replete with examples illustrating the positive outcomes ensuing from their engagement with their son's learning. In Australia, Fletcher and Dally (2002) offer a meta-view of the international dimension of fathers and children's pre-school literacy development which suggests that whilst men are generally more reluctant to participate in print-related activities, the net benefits of their doing so are substantial. Similarly, Fagan (1999) in the United States has reported the positive impact of fathers' involvement in education programmes for preschool children, whilst Nord, Brimholl and West (1997) used data drawn from almost 17,000 children and young people to highlight the benefits of paternal involvement.

This brief glimpse of some of the recent research on fathers and sons enables us to make several overview observations. Firstly, that relatively little is written about 'non problematic' fathering, in the sense that there appears to be an absence of focus in the literature which addresses the experiences of fathers and sons in 'successful' and productive relationships. The tendency instead to problematise is perhaps linked to the dilemmas surrounding paternal roles as a result of changed social and cultural attitudes to masculinity (Martino and Mayenn, 2001), to increasingly varied fathering lifestyles (Lee, 2005) and to attention being directed to family factors as explanations of anti-social or challenging behaviour amongst boys (Spielberg, 1999). And yet, somewhat perversely, it would also be fair to view the present volume as contributing to this literature imbalance, given that much of its content is directed at the 'difficulty' in fathering and in being a son.

But whilst the focus of research seems to be the crisis-dimension of being a father and son, the summary message of the associated research studies point to a set of imperatives for the role of fathers in fostering the well-being of their sons. Thus, the involvement of fathers in their sons' education, in the broadest sense of the term, is associated with:

- less alcohol and other drug use and less delinquency, and violent behaviour among adolescent boys (Zimmerman, Salem and Notaro, 2000)
- adolescent boys whose fathers are more involved in their schooling being less likely to be delinquent (Zimmerman, Salem and Notaro, 2000)
- less depression amongst male adolescents when there is greater paternal involvement (Caldwell, Antonucci and Jackson, 1997)
- closer involvement by boys with fathers helps to insulate them against risk factors for violence (Zimmerman, Steinman, and Rowe, 1998)
- less substance abuse and depression when more time is spent with the father (Zimmerman, Salem and Notaro, 2000)

When education in its formal sense is considered, two sets of advantages are firmly evidenced in the literature. Firstly, there is now a systematic body of research which points to the raising of achievement levels amongst boys when there is closer involvement on the part of their fathers (as summarised, for instance, by Green, 2003 and by Goldman, 2004). Secondly, there are demonstrable associations between the level of father's participation in their son's education and their 'at-risk' status with regard to delinquency and subsequent criminality (Flouri *et al*, 2004).

Consideration of these issues can be scrutinised more closely, a process which affirms the importance of the growing level of interest in the role of men – and more particularly fathers – in the education of their sons.

Some considerations for practitioners

At first sight it would appear that relatively little has been researched or written about the status of fathers and sons within education but this would be somewhat misleading. Whilst it is certainly true that there is a shortage of both research and scholarship relating to fathers and their sons compared to the volume of material on, for example, parents or care-givers generally, it is possible to identify some rich strands of work which offer excellent insights and suggestions to practitioners. One of the difficulties in accessing these resources is that they comprise a quite disparate collection, from a variety of professional or academic orientations, prompted as they have been by interest groups, funding agencies or governments often operating in apparent isolation. These are referred to in the course of the substantive chapters in this book.

There is, in addition to these sources, evidence of a need to obtain greater knowledge, including research data, on a range of issues which are absolutely germane to the enhancement of professional relationships with fathers and sons in the 21st century. In other words, whilst there is a corpus of knowledge which serves certain academic functions, professionals interfacing directly with fathers and sons might benefit from a more focused and specific set of studies.

Conversations with teachers, child-care professionals and some parents reveals a range of possible themes for enquiry, practical activity or evaluation, and which might usefully inform an agenda to promote both information-capture and professional development in this important field:

- father's biographies and educational careers
- father-friendly schools
- fathers as mentors in schools
- sons and fathers 'working together' in classrooms
- excluded pupils and the role of fathers
- teacher-shadowing by fathers
- fathers-and-boys clubs
- 'father-line' communication
- male-orientated curriculum development
- father involvement in 'SEAL' curricula inputs

- greater involvement of men in Parent Partnerships
- studies of resilience factors relating to 'effective fathering'
- father-friendly home-school communications

This is clearly an incomplete list. It has been generated in an *ad hoc* fashion from no more than nine individuals with an involvement in the field. Nonetheless, it does point to the multi-dimensional scope of potential knowledge gathering regarding father-and-son involvement in schools and in education.

4

'Wait 'til your Dad gets home'. Fathers, masculinity and role(play)

I was always fearful of disapproval and looked warily from the gabled-window of my Church Lane bunker for the Cortina to swing through the wrought-iron gates, the Check-Point Charlie fending off the world and keeping us private. We all, as kids, wondered what mood he'd be in. We became judge and jury, delivering an instant verdict before his brogues touched the driveway. I wanted so much to please him. I wanted to be all those things in the classroom that he never had the chance to be. I remember these things with great clarity and it made me be who I was in the classroom. I needed to do well at school. I wanted to be his successful son. Dad was never omnipresent in my own education like my mother, who orchestrated school homework in the manner of a dictator in my developing world. But failing for her seemed more comfortable as it was insulated by the duvet of her understanding. Apprehension was usually at its height when the sun shone down – I have never really understood why. Maybe a day spent humdrum driving to meet the miscellanies of corrugated garages styled as 'motor factors', inhabiting a masculine world to which he scarcely belonged, took it out of him. No mobile 'phone or CD distractions: the Cortina was his metal hell or heaven dependent on how the mood was. And looking, on this day of recall, from my window I saw signs as I sometimes did – of a father wanting to talk to his son, but walking backwards from that encounter in the face of an embarrassed absence of what he called 'an education [A]

My father as a pupil was how he was as a man. Born not made? Of that I can't be sure, although I am sure that I am made from him. I like to think I've got a side of me that can be 'feminine', in touch with all the things that fathers today are supposed to be in touch with. But, though I'll nod quite smugly in that direction from time to time, I know deep down that I function just like he did – my role is to decide, to arbitrate, to agree-to, and to always be strong in doing those things [A]

You've got to say that in this day and age the time when the man was the boss of the house is long gone ... I'd say anyway. I mean, we both go out to work, and she works longer hours than me as well. I don't think my lad sees me the same way as I looked at my own Dad. He was the real head of the house and you wouldn't want to get on his wrong side. Maybe because of that he had a lot more kind of ... well ... he didn't see himself as superior, but I'd say he was a definite 'father-figure' ... not sure you'd say that about me. Then again, I was quite distant with my Dad ... he had his pub mates, didn't talk too much with me and my brother. Well, he did about the usual boy-men things ... football, cricket ... we used to have good fun watching boxing late at night after Mum had gone to bed [B]

Being a father is a natural thing for me and most of the guys I know. It's not as though it's the number one topic of conversation, it just sort of happens, if you get my meaning. I never thought too much about it really, not that much at all until now, as you've asked about it ... and I think that as blokes we can be a bit ... I think you give anyone who you're having a drink ... you know, socialising or things like that. Well, it may sound bad to someone like you, but I think you'd be a bit suspicious of a bloke who gets to our age and has never had kids ... I'd be definitely thinking, you know, non pc and all that stuff, but definitely, he's bowling for the other side [B]

My Dad's OK. He gets in some big moods sometimes but I can cope with that because I just stay in my room and play music ... stuff like that. He doesn't very often, but when he's in one you have to watch it. We all do, careful ... right? I understand him. Me and him. We've been in big rows and he's got a red face and starts spitting. But I do ... I'd say ... really understand him ... being angry, where it all comes from. And it's dead funny because the more angry he gets I know he'll never hit me. He's never done that. In the end I'm sure he goes behind a door and starts laughing. Sometimes we've laughed out loud about it ... but that's why we understand each other, right? That's his style, way of doing things and that's why we have this ... understanding ... We watch the Rangers, his team ... done it for years and years and it gives us time, well, boys-time I'd say. It's good really. We go the pub before it (football) and I get a half or a pint of shandy. He knows people which is strange because round us, our house and that, he doesn't talk much. But he's got humour and I like it when he's like that ... popular, because it reflects on me, right? You don't want your mates to see your Dad as a sad old geezer do you? No, you'd not want it at all [C]

I get by alright, just about. I do my thing and he does his. That's how we are now, because I'm older. And I prefer that, I've got mates and I hang out with them. So we don't see much of each other ... not all that much anymore. And it works that way really because I'm sometimes, well, I know I am sometimes a bit of a stroppy bastard ... I can get a bit ... do things that are stupid and that, and then we'll have a row. We wind each other up a bit ... I think he finds it hard to see me as getting older now, being a man like him [C]

Themes highlighted by the fathers and sons in their narratives:

- sons need their fathers to be seen as 'good dads'
- fathers as decision-makers
- changing roles and status of dads
- the positive experiences of having children (sons)
- surviving unsatisfactory/abusive relationships
- sons and fathers struggling to adjust to adolescence

Attention has been drawn in recent years to an apparent 'crisis' in the way that masculinity is expressed, both in boys and in men. We have already pointed to some of the issues emerging as a result of this in our introduction and context-setting. An overview of contemporary understandings of adult masculinity suggest that it is characterised by dilemmas and uncertainties in many areas of male 'being' – their role in families, in employment, in general society and especially in their personal relationships within families and beyond them. Boys inhabit an equally uncertain territory, exacerbated by their struggle to construct an identity as a child or young person in the absence of a clear model of what 'being male' should be – and, adding further complexity, a long-standing problem of effectively defining the parameters of childhood itself (Aries, 1962; Hymowitz, 1999). As a result, both fathers and their sons have to forge new masculine identities. This difficult process is further complicated by the impact of cultural, racial and social class factors (Pattman, Frosh and Phoenix, 1998; Sewell, 1996). And, without doubt, the impact of such role reassignments on boys has important implications for teachers and others working in schools.

There are important historical precedents in the study of male identity in respect of education and the world of work. Here one thinks of such seminal studies as Willis (1977) and Corrigan (1979), both of which portrayed male culture as oppositional, sexist and inclined to use violence to deal with problematic situations. Such interpretations, whilst having their place in providing some important snapshot information regarding boys' attitudes to schooling, did not really come to grips with the relationship dimensions of their existence. Moreover, these were very particular studies, which suggest that the 'problem' of masculinity was something that was implicit to certain specific cultural or social groups (in the case of Willis's work, for example, the 'lads') who were marginalised or presented difficulties on account of their educational underachievement or unacceptable social behaviours.

More recent studies tend to locate the tensions and dilemmas of masculinity as an issue of gender. As such it has an impact across male communities, being viewed as generic to masculine culture as a whole, not just to father and son relationships. Problems which are applicable to the entire gender group, therefore, relate variously to such things as an absence of appropriate positive male role models in schools (Pollack, 1998), differences in preferred learning and social-interaction styles (Jackson, 1998) and so on. Recent developments in researching masculinity have highlighted the need to see this as comprising multiple, rather than a single, masculine identities.

So how is 'masculinity' constructed, cross-referenced and grown in a father-son relationship? A starting point in interrogating this is to consider whether there is evidence that sons inherit their father's personality traits and performances. This question, with its 'chip off the old block' characterisations, has been an ongoing theme of enquiry over many years. What we are reasonably assured of is that, whilst environmental effects substantially reinforce personality tendencies, there remain important genetic continuities which need to be at least acknowledged and incorporated into a multi-factorial explanation of masculine identity formation. As Eaves *et al* (1999) indicate, 'The significant contribution of genetic factors to social attitudes means that virtually no measurable aspect of human behavioural variation is so far removed from the impact of events at the genetic level as to be considered in complete isolation from the emerging theory and knowledge in genetics and sociobiology' (Eaves *et al*, 1999). In fact, across a range of father-son activities (whether these be 'normal' pro-social actions or delinquent or criminal activities) there is a consensual view that, notwithstanding a very small number of exceptionalities, both environmental and biological factors influence the emergence of the 'masculine' in fathers and sons.

Fathers, of course, play an integral role in formulating and regulating the emotional response – itself linked to all kinds of educational and social behaviours – of their sons. The very young child's early experiences of this are usually made through their principal caregivers – usually mothers, but sometimes fathers (Crokenberg and Leerkes, 2005). They do this through 'social referencing' – or looking to their mother or father for emotional guidance (Klinnert, 1984). The adults' facial expressions and simple verbal cues influence the behaviour by the child. Recent research in this area has revealed an increasingly wide range of social-referencing behaviour amongst parents (Mumme, Fernald and Herrara, 1996).

Social referencing can be both positive and negative. Parents will display 'approach behaviours' which include looking directly at the child and touching them or their favourite toy. Conversely, 'avoidant behaviours' characterise negative social referencing, and are exemplified by looking away from the child and actually avoiding contact with the favourite toy. From a gender perspective it is interesting that there is little evidence of any distinction between the social referencing by mothers and fathers (Hirshberg and Svejda, 1990). This does seem unusual, given that fathers, including some of those who have contributed to the narrative formulations in this book, are aware of a tendency to avoid eye contact or the use of positive, affirming language. It seems logical, then, to question whether these fathers have failed to develop social-referencing skills beyond those they demonstrate during the early nurturing of their sons.

The role of the father in the development of 'gender identity' has not been substantially researched (Zucker and Bradley, 2005). The American Psychiatric Association's diagnostic manual DSM-IV identifies gender identity disorder (GID) as 'a strong and persistent cross-gender identification' (APA, 2000) characterised by such things as cross-dressing, a desire to engage in stereotypical games of the other gender and a strong preference for playmates of the other sex. GID is also delineated by 'persistent discomfort with his or her sex or sense of in appropriateness in the gender role of that sex' (*ibid*). Green (1987) found that paternal separation occurred earlier in the families of GID boys. The same author also pointed out that fathers of GID boys (whether present in the home or non-resident-fathers) recalled spending little time with their sons.

Fathers have particular opportunities to influence their son's regulatory behaviour – for example, fathers are more inclined to participate in rough-and-tumble play (Crockenberg and Leerkes, 2005). What is therefore surprising is that the father's contribution to their child's emotional regulation has scarcely been the focus of research (Parke and Tinsley, 1987). But there are some useful studies which point to this as a fruitful area of enquiry for father-son relationships. Power and Parke (1983), for example, indicate that fathers are inclined to lack sensitivity towards their son's emotional 'signals' during the course of physical play, and they see this as potentially contributing to a failure by the child to regulate his behaviour. In contrast, Volling *et al* (1998) demonstrated that when fathers were more sensitive and less intrusive in physical play, their 12-month old infants were generally more emotionally competent.

Some considerations for practitioners

The most obvious issues for professionals working with and for fathers and sons discussed in this chapter – notably relating to role-status, adjustment to change and the perceptions of sons about their dads – are addressed elsewhere in this book.

5

'In my day ... .'
Fathers and sons as pupils

My father as a pupil was how he was as a man. Born not made? Of that I can't be sure, although I am sure that I am made from him. Periodically – well, more frequently than that – I am immersed in regret and personal retribution that I scarcely talked with him about his own days in school. And he would seldom talk of who he was as a pupil at Higher Broughton County School, in the old Salford Education Committee. Anecdotes punctuated any conversation, but that's all they were then: disjointed snapshots of a schooling which was scarcely satisfactory even then – and much, much less so now. When I arrived at university, having benefited from the indulgences of both my parents, I soon realised that I didn't know much about him as a learner in school, save those occasional stories extracted in fireside conversations. Although I have felt it increasingly in recent years, as my own sons grow, I even then knew that I wasn't getting the full story [A]

Fred Carrack was his head-teacher. His immaculate script summarised nine years of education in what was mysteriously (and yet I suspect indelicately) called the 'Mixed Department' of the school, ending as it did on June 27, 1932. The fanfare for his personality and character was loud and amplified by Mr Beard his classteacher. The phrases roll benevolently from pen to paper in the manner of a male Miss Brodie: 'All I can say of him is to his credit', whilst 'His honesty, diligence and enthusiasm is above question'. It was, of course. And as a Dad he manfully made the most of those things [A]

I had a rubbish time. School was the place I'd go to see my mates. I know from quite early that there'd be no point in exams or owt like that. It wasn't as if I didn't care either. I did. I wanted things. But in the end like a lot of others I threw in the towel ... you know ... gave up. There was a pecking order ... usually no lads ... none of my mates ... were there. If you were a girl you'd be alright except if you were a slapper like Sandra________ They'd got her sussed ... and I think old Messer [teacher's nick-name_____________] fancied her too and had no respect. But yeah, girls. Remember Greavsie? Shit, he was a girl, a nerdy alright and I'll bet that all of 'em like that'd do alright. Nah, can't say that school did much for me ... a couple of CSEs but who'd want that? My lad's going to be different ... well, at least, I think it's different now. I've only got the wife's say so on that. She looks after that side of things me being away an' that. I'm not good in school. It worries me, makes me feel ... that I'm still there, you know, small. I did go one time but, well ... you've got this twenty-year old just out from college telling you this and that about your own kid. It's not on isn't that. Can't say I'm all that keen to go back

I try and show an interest, but a lot of the stuff he's doing is like a different language to me. He's just started at secondary [school]. He's still a child and yet I can't get to grips with what he's doing ... no, I understand it, you know, all of the nuts and bolts stuff, the knowledge like ... it's just the way he's learning, that's what really does my head in. If it were left to me to say, I'd definitely tell you that it's not proper learning, all that ... it's just not like it should be, in my view [B]

The thing I always look back on when I think of my own lad in school is how much input my own folks put in to my education ... they were like a second and a third teacher really. My mother was the most obvious person, and she'd be the one that'd always make sure I got down to it ... [homework]. But I seem to remember my Dad doing his bit band being really annoyed with me if I came across as though I wasn't interested or started to fool about with my brother [B]

He'll sometimes really kick off into the 'life-in-my-day' routine. I love it, all that stuff. It's like Eastenders, him carrying on about how it was this and that. Just like looking at the TV ... might as well be. It's all a big hard-luck story, how he'd do things different, how he wished he'd had this opportunity or that one ... it's all down to me, it all comes at me, that stuff. I'm living it all again for him. We should change places, then he could have things he never did have, that'd surprise him, definitely. It's a load of bollocks as well ... all that stuff because it's nothing at all to do with me now, trying to get qualifications, a job and all that. It's all about him, me, me, me, me, me ... Yes, that's it ... he's had one go at it and now, like a big spoilt kid, he wants another. Well, fuck it, he's not having mine [C]

He was the recipient of what is still referred to in oxymoronic mode as a 'good, old-fashioned education' and I think that he, and millions of fathers like him over the years, have come to regard that schooling as a cornerstone for their lives. Of course, a large section of the male community has looked the other way, but there's something there which suggests to me that school was at that time a place where a very particular, traditional form of masculinity was played out [C]

Themes highlighted by the fathers and sons in their narratives:

- importance of knowing one's own dad
- respecting 'histories'
- impact of unhappy schooling on father-son relationship
- father's struggling to understand 'new' ways of learning
- living another life through a son
- the challenge of physically connecting with schools

To what extent is a father's engagement with school based on their own experiences of being in school? Evidence suggests that this is an important factor in home-school relationships generally, but that it comes to have greater significance in cases where a child is marginalised on account, for example of inappropriate behaviour or by having a particular learning difficulty. In these cases, too, there is some evidence of co-morbidity between the educational performance of the child and that of the father. It is not difficult to see why the father-school interface in such cases can at times be tense and difficult.

One starting point, then, is a father's own school experiences and school performances. A link has been established between the educational and social performance of boys in school and that of their parents – especially their father – before them. Research dating back over 40 years indicates that the educational performance of pupils in school is associated by teachers with their father's social class, itself then being further linked to the level of achievement by the father (Goodacre, 1968). Douglas (1964), in what has come to be viewed as a classic piece of research on 'the home and the school' makes the point that educational aspirations of working-class fathers correlates strongly with their performance levels. Douglas points out the subsequent lack of contact with school amongst working-class fathers, compared to those he defines as 'middle class', stating (albeit generically) that 'The middle-class parents take more interest in their children's progress at school than the manual working-class parents do, and they become relatively more interested as their children grow older' (p.81).

Whilst taking into account the obvious changes that have been assimilated in the way that we now deal with class as an issue in education, Douglas's summary points us in the direction of two issues for discussion. The first is the cyclical nature of fathers' involvement in their son's schooling, a process in which parental underachievement appears to be linked to their relative lack of social and economic capital and which is then associated with them failing to value 'getting an education'. The reverberations on the academic progress of the son are such that a similar pattern of perception and belief about the importance of school is established – resulting in further under-performance.

A second inference to be drawn from these distal data is that the unsatisfactory experiences in learning at school has created in the mind of the father a degree of reluctance to engage with anything which for them is a painful reminder of an unhappy aspect of their upbringing. An extreme manifestation of this is reported by Martin *et al* (1999) who showed that school-phobia in the father was readily transferred to the son. Similar correlations are inferred by McShane, Walter and Rey, (2001). At a somewhat lesser level of severity, Brighouse (1985) observes that 'The memories of many parents of school are of places surrounded by high walls bedecked by embedded broken glass with no school noticeboard beyond the one discouraging the entrance of their parents' and that many would also have a perception of schools as '... an island, where the young are initiated by teachers who are almost the equivalent of witch-doctors' (p.153). With such overwhelming recollections, it is hardly surprising that some fathers are disinclined to subject themselves to revisiting such memories.

Parental involvement in schools has a long if somewhat erratic history in England, as elsewhere. The historical emergence of the role of parents in schools has been charted by Hurt (1985). The last twenty years have seen a surge in interest amongst politicians, administrators and practitioners in the participation of parents in schools. Legislation, major reports and guidance documents have all set out both the duty and requirements of schools to engage parents in the education of their children. In spite of these initiatives there may still be a negative residue from the previous period, so that some parents hold views about schools which result in a form of adult alienation which echoes their childhood experience. This has important implications for practitioners – making schools boy friendly by promoting more involvement from fathers is a vital task for the future.

Some considerations for practitioners

Some schools are taking practical steps towards creating learning and social environments which provide extended opportunities for boys to succeed. Inevitably they implicate fathers as key partners in the enterprise. Information and action needs to be forthcoming at two levels: firstly, that which relates to the school as an educational organisation; and secondly, initiatives which focus on fathers themselves.

At school level it is helpful to conduct an audit of provision so as to assess exactly how boy friendly the school actually is. One extremely helpful initiative is the Family Action Centre's *Boys in Schools Program* (2007). This sets out ten questions which enable the school climate to be evaluated in relation to boy's learning. These can act both as a checklist and as the basis for an action plan:

- Does the school publish/utilise data regarding boy's progress?
- Does the school identify boys specifically in its mission and action statements?
- How does the school promote the developmental, social and learning needs of boys in its teaching and assessment?

- How does the school cater for the different learning needs of boys (and girls)?
- What is the principles and processes of/for staff recruitment?
- How are boys involved in decision-making?
- How are boys who are shy, overweight, 'arty' or 'middle-band' recognised and celebrated?
- Does the school have an explicit strategy for involving Dads?
- Is part of the staff development programme directed towards boys/fathers?

Such a schedule of information-gathering and action should at least be prompted by pragmatism. There is a wealth of evidence, referred to in this book, of the relationship between educational performance amongst boys and their preferred learning styles. Similarly, where boys are engaged learners there is a corresponding body of evidence suggesting that they are less inclined to misbehave in classrooms. And, finally, the 'pull' factor of boy friendly schools is a significant factor in overcoming non-attendance.

There are broader benefits for the school as an inclusive learning environment too, as well as for society at large. Engaging boys, who will mostly become fathers themselves, more actively and wholeheartedly in their own schooling presents a great opportunity to break at least one of the cycles of disadvantage that punctuates education and the society of which it is an expression.

There has been some policy focus, together with accompanying practical advice, addressed directly to fathers – though it is uncertain whether such initiatives are likely to be accessed by the groups of 'marginalised' Dads that form such a major element of this book. One such tranche of advice is that proffered by the *Family and Parenting Institute* (2006); this covers a range of highly practical advice which, importantly, is communicated in a straightforward and accessible way.

6

Fathers and early nurturing

There's a lot of questions you ask yourself, you know, about whether you're doing the right thing ... I think men do that a lot more now than when I was a kid. My Dad knew what was what, he had a role, he just got on with it. I'm sure he wouldn't sit there and be asked questions by somebody like you, he'd have no time for it. He needn't have because nobody thought that there's a problem. Mind you, with the divorces and stuff it's a lot more complicated. Divorce when I was a lad was a talking point, I'd hear me Dad with me Mam, talking about somebody ... it was talk of the town, was divorce. The tele has got a lot to answer for an' all. When I'm on lates I'll watch the daytime and there'll be this and that know-it-all telling you what's needed ... how to bring your kid up right. It give you an inferiority ... at least, it would if you took it seriously [A]

My Dad cuddled me. I remember. It tickled. He tickled. It was good. I heard him. Laughing. He scratched but that was his beard ... it was stubbly and sometimes it hurt a bit. He did it when he came in. We were all in bed, sometimes asleep. I'd hear him on the stairs ... footsteps and I'd hide ... and ... get down in the sheets. It was like a game and I'd pretend I was asleep. Those were the best bits ... the bits when he thought I was asleep, and he'd still reach over and give ... a kiss. I wanted him to do it again, his breath ... all stinky, but don't mind. He'd come in to me. I don't know. It makes me sad a lot now to think he'll never do it again [A]

You can transfer all sorts of anxieties, You become yourself again through your child. How to neutralise this transference. It is problematic because I definitely wanted the good bits of me to be recycled. But then, we're not all that good at recognising or being overt about our positive qualities, strengths. And I reckon the more introspective you are or become, the more likely it is that only the unsatisfactory things are brought out from the basement of your head. That's when it gets really ugly: I know that some of the quite awful personality traits that I have nurtured as a big part of me have already found their way along the father-son pipeline. I see them, played out before me as inept or sometimes more unflattering still. And as a father am I supposed to admonish, to correct or sanction? Even at my most crass I am able to see the sense of irony in all of that. That I'm about to punish the lad for being me. It's a theatre of fools, a one act play to depict what not to do. And yet, most dads do, I'd say [B]

I sometimes wonder whether I'd have been better having the first boy much later. I was naïve and completely unfinished, and most people who I met as a new Dad were able to tell. I was more connected I think with private worlds of my own feelings and emotions, rather than a more public connection with the boy. Yes, I am pretty sure that I loved him, but I don't think that I did enough to demonstrate that affection I felt towards him. It was more than that. It was a feeling of absolute joy at having him there, around me. I loved the smell, the feeds, the nappies. I was connected at that mundane level [B]

Before we had him I was a typical lad ... you know, sharing her-indoors jokes with me mates, telling each other who'd lay the law down, what we'd do and not do. And I wasn't young, thinking back ... 22, 23 that sort of age ... and yet there'd be all sorts of pub-talk about it ... it's very different though now, much more different than I ever thought it was going to be ... I mean, who'd have guessed that somebody like me, a bit you know, well, a bit out there, lairy whatever ... who'd have guessed that I'd be insisting, yes ... absolutely insisting ... that it was me who'd change his nappy? No question, you know, of turn and turn about, no. And I think I'm the one who worries a lot as well ... no, I'm not saying she doesn't but ... well, whatever, I don't know but I still think I worry that bit more because he's my boy. It has surprised me a lot, how I've taken to it, how I've really come to be a Dad, you know. I get involved, love it really ... [B]

Dad always used to be the last up to tuck me in. It was nice. I would listen for him coming and I'd wait for it. I used to leave a football or army book on my bed so that he'd pick it up, and I could show him things. It usually worked. Sometimes we'd sit for ages just looking through one of the books [C]

I can't remember anything as far back as that ... not with my Dad I can't. Most of the things I remember are not good. I remember being sad sometimes, because my Dad never seemed to be there, and I missed it. The others all had proper Dads, holding his hand, playing games, football ... Mine was a Dad whenever he felt like it [C]

Themes highlighted by the fathers and sons in their narratives:

- de-skilling fathers
- 'anxious' fathering
- importance of emotional closeness, touch
- lack of confidence in their child-rearing skills
- the challenge of being a 'young' father
- sons want physical and emotional closeness

Historically it is fair to suggest that the stereotype was that of the mother's dominance as the principal carer, and such a view is still deep-seated, although nevertheless undergoing considerable change in the last thirty or so years (Smith, 1995). As recently as the 1950s the father was largely excluded from what Hostler (1953) called 'the magic circle of mother and child'. Any nurturing involvement by the father was often met by quizzical or patronising responses, as Smith (1995) observes. The 100 or so years up to the 1970s were characterised by a perceptible de-skilling of fathers, as more and more of the central functions of the family have gradually been usurped by state agencies – whether in terms of socialisation by such initiatives as the current citizenship agenda of central government or child-care as, for example, in 'extended schools'. Indeed, some commentators insist that very little has changed, apart from a superficial involvement of fathers in some policy initiatives; Burgess and Ruxton (1996) talk about the continued 'cultural alienation' of fathers. They suggest that most representations of fatherhood are negative, fathers being seen as absent, irrelevant, deviant or criminal, incompetent or abusive. This is highlighted by Deven (1994) in a survey of media coverage of fathers.

But Smith (1995) adopts a more optimistic position, noting the emergence of studies in the 1970s and 1980s which sought to explore fathers' feelings and emotions about 'being a father'. Several factors have possibly influenced this perceived incremental shift in attitudes during the last thirty years. One is attendance at childbirth, allowing an almost immediate physical bond to form between son and father. This is well illustrated by data from the Avon Longitudinal Study of Pregnancy and Childhood (ALSPAC, 2006), which charts the dramatic increase in paternal attendance at childbirth between the 1950s (5%) through the 1970s (35%) to the 1990s (97%) in a sample cohort of almost 300 fathers. As already mentioned, changes in employment patterns mean that a greater number of mothers of young children now go out to work; consequently more households share early child-caring responsibilities. It is worth adding as a footnote the feminist critique of the greater involvement of fathers in domestic child-rearing: that it is a means by which men can further dominate women by invading an area which has traditionally been the preserve of the mother.

Dads play an essential role in parenting. Evidence from research in many countries is certainly explicit in defining the clear connection between the involvement of the natural father and a child's educational, psychological and social outcomes. The role of the father as a positive depiction of male participation in the family and all that is connected with its maintenance is vital in establishing effective male interactions and relationships in future years. And yet it is equally accurate to point to a number of inhibiting factors which prevent many fathers who want to be more centrally involved with their sons from being able to do so.

Whalley (2003) refers to the difficulties experienced in getting in touch with the fathers of very young children. She writes: '... in several cases fathers had no contact with their biological children. In other cases, when parents had separated acrimoniously, fathers were not informed about what was happening in their children's lives at nursery' (pp.27-28). She also refers to the gate-keeping function of the mother, who acted as a censor of information coming into the home from the nursery or child-care setting. And even when there has been some success in involving fathers there remains problems in sustaining such inputs over longer periods of time.

One explanation for the relative lack of father-involvement in formal early years provision is that such programmes have been, historically, the preserve of women. In the United States, for instance, 97 per cent of workers involved in pre-kindergarten programmes were women (CCCW, 2002), whilst Sanders (2002) notes the 'overwhelmingly female' employment profile in this sector. Wardle (2007) indicates the wish of fathers to be respected as equal partners in child-rearing and to feel able to talk directly to them about their children without consistently deferring to their wives or partners. But the gendered nature of early child-care settings can cause men to enter a 'zone difference' (Sanders, 2002) and the resulting cultural conflict makes them experiencing feelings of isolation and marginalisation. The additional likelihood, noted by Fagan (1996), that many female workers may themselves be single parents who might have strong feelings of resentment towards fathers can exacerbate matters.

All of these factors which play a part in creating either a real or apparent distancing in a father's engagement with their child are compounded by the high visibility that fathers tend to have when child protection issues are considered. These fathers have been identified as representative of both the youngest and the oldest fathers: Egan-Sage and Carpenter (1999) suggest that either an absence of key parenting skills (young fathers) or less-tolerant and disciplinarian parenting styles (older fathers) contribute to their over-representation on the child-protection register. Certainly, there is abundant research evidence to highlight men's reluctance to embark on careers in early years teaching and child-care. Kitzinger (1988) has even noted that contemporary society is inclined to view men caring for children as 'slightly deviant'.

Some considerations for practitioners

The involvement of fathers in the early stages of child-rearing is absolutely vital to the healthy emotional and social development of all children. It is particularly important for boys, as the literature identified has indicated. There are substantial attitudinal and structural constraints to the growth of this involvement, notwithstanding the progress made in some settings in England and elsewhere – the 'long hours' culture and the shifts in employment patterns are two such inhibitors. In spite of this it is fair to acknowledge that one of the most extensive surveys of fathers (EOC, 2002) revealed that, far from wanting less involvement in the early nurturing of their child, fathers actually stated a desire for a more equal share in child-care responsibilities. Early child-care settings, as well as infant schools, need to develop approaches which allow fathers to become more centrally involved: all the recent research noted in this chapter points to this being implicated positively in the pro-social and academic development of boys.

Conversations with fathers on the topic of their involvement in early nurturing are revealing. They suggest that in spite of the many local initiatives that are currently being progressed relating to boys and men (see, for instance, those summarised by *The Trust for the Study of Adolescence* (2007), fathers continue to express feelings of marginalisation. Thus when this small reference group were asked what prevented them from accessing existing activities at nursery or infant school there was widespread agreement that:

- these Dads lacked information about activities
- some Dads indicated that any information sent to the home was invariably addressed to the mother
- some Dads indicated an uncertainty about many school activities being only for women
- several Fathers indicated that they felt 'out-of-place' and 'uncomfortable' in the presence of (mainly) women
- the employment circumstances of these Fathers, and especially when their work-hours, did not allow for participation
- these Fathers were very positive about wanting greater involvement in their sons' education and welcomed suggestions about participating in play-school events, coffee-mornings and so on.

Kahn (2006) conducted a recent study which explicitly targets fathers for the *Pre-school Learning Alliance*. Using a sample of 29 early-years settings, the study examined the efficacy of four models for promoting father-involvement in their child's education. These comprised (1) Inclusive Communication which highlighted the need for settings to ensure that their communications to parents were father friendly, in that communications with the home used language that specifically appealed to men; (2) Father Directed Activities which concentrated attention on organising activities that would appeal specifically to fathers; (3) GenderTalk which concentrates on encouraging discussion about roles and expectations as a precursor to the greater involvement of fathers and; (4) a Leaflet Only approach, in which participant Fathers were given a copy of a bespoke *Fathers Matter* leaflet.

The implications of Kahn's findings are vital, both for fathers and for those working in early-years settings. The report recommended training sessions to develop an awareness of fathers as participants in early child-care. It also proposed the formulation of local action plans to involve fathers; and a booklet with incorporating exemplary case studies of 'What Works in Involving Fathers'. The study also offered practical advice relating to the importance of retaining updated records about the composition of families, and incorporating information on fathers living apart from their children.

Kahn also provides advice about the need to communicate explicitly with fathers and mothers whilst recognising their generic roles as parents or carer. The study recommends that staff working in early-years settings should be pro-active in engaging with fathers when they collect and drop off their children, especially in instances where this might be the main or only contact point with Fathers.

As with other Father-and-son related activity, what Kahn's work illustrates is the beginnings of both policy and practice activity in addressing issues which have, for some time, remained as scarcely tangential issues for many early-year practitioners. By engaging Fathers more actively in formal early-years education it seems entirely likely that accrued benefits will be realised beyond the settings in which they are undertaken. A greater commitment towards a recognising fathers as essential participants in the early education of their sons will bring a broader set of societal benefits, as Nord, Brimhall and West (1997) note.

7

Being a teaching dad: trials and tribulations

Yes, my father was a teacher ... well, actually he was a headteacher when I was 14 ... it was not as bad a situation as you'd think now. There wasn't any bullying, nothing like that ... which I suppose makes it different to the situation nowadays. But there was a bit of mickey-taking, that sort of thing, nothing nasty, just with your classmates mainly. It was a bit odd though when you looked up on the stage at assembly and there was your Dad. That was quite weird, especially if there was something serious he had to say ... and I'd be thinking, last night, we were down the sailing club, both together, and we'd been having a great time, a laugh ... now he was serious, very stern and ... different [A]

There was this freaky time, really crazy time ... I coped with it OK because I was little ... I mean, I was still in shorts, still at primary ... Dad had just started his teacher training course ... he'd been in the Army for six years, left and ... he was well, he came into my class, just sitting there with some others ... I kept looking at him, he pretended not to see me, but I know he did [A]

Every child matters? Is that really the case? Jimmy didn't matter at all. Wire-hair and tousled-top. I remember it all. The to-and-fro action to comfort the already lonely soul, the snuggle against a protective cot-side. He took so long to eat that first digestive biscuit. It was, to state the obvious, his security and he gripped tight enough to make it finally disintegrate. Oh Jimmy. Did you matter? – I'll keep asking in the hope that I'll get a different answer. There is always time, when raising kids, to reflect on what might have been and so it should be because it can help to light up a different future. My own recollections are unclear, not because I can't 'see it', but because my picture of those years is obscured by the tears of regret that continue to fall whenever I think of my seaweed-trousered boy, alone and eating sand and trying to become a son for me. And in my professional detachment and the arrogance of my then still mystical youth I failed to use my energy, skills and social capital to buy him anything of a future. I contributed to a casualty in just as systematic a way as the studied indifference of an abuser's accomplice: knowing it was happening and not doing enough, not measuring up. I was part of the problem. And, I suppose, many of the Dad's like me, caught-out, paralysed between parenthood and professionalism, cannot fail to see the irony of it all [B]

I still incline a fretful gaze at school transport – those slightly ageing Transits, unmarked normally apart from a child safety logo on the rear. I look past toughened-glass at the eyes of the toughening faces, transported as they are on a daily basis to their educational abattoirs. Jim had big sad eyes, although to be accurate his was a yellow bus, belching diesel as it fought its way up past Kellet church to oblivion. Yes, they were magnified and remain just so, surveying as he did then the discontented fatherhood and telling me with those eyes that I really can do better than this. And yet he still went on that bus, an ignominious statement of my own bankrupt fatherhood [B]

It gives you a better insight into how your lad is doing, but I don't think I could teach him all the time. He's seen me in too many other different, informal situations and I think that'd worry me ... and I think it's also very unfair ... well, it would be unfair ... on him because I think it'd mean his position in his peer group would be very unusual. I mean, that being said I haven't gone to the head and said could he try not to timetable me for his classes ... nothing as daft as that ... but, you'll understand my point, it would be tough sometimes leaving 'Dad' behind and become Mr Wavell ... the teacher [B]

He was dead awkward. But I liked that, because it showed we'd got a relationship. It was only for a year but then he left. He got another job. But my mates did think ... well, they said to me, 'it must be good with your Dad as a teacher because ... ' and it was all about getting away with things, getting out of homework and that ... and him putting in an excuse for me ... But I wasn't a nerd or the teacher's pet. No nothing like that. It was the opposite and I think ... I'm sure ... some people made it hard for me ... tried to make me suffer. Not the kids, the teachers ... who'd have thought that? [C]

I like it when Dad does a cover lesson. All my mates know that he's my father and it's really cool. They don't mess about, I think they like it because he must come across, in their head, as more as one of us ... because I'm his son, stuff like that. He doesn't really say much to me at all, though. We've got a bet, amongst us, that he'll deffo say 'Wait until I you get you home!' ... I'm sure he will, one day, just for a laugh [C]

Themes highlighted by the fathers and sons in their narratives:

- potential relationship tensions
- feelings of guilt, regret and inadequacy
- peer-allegiances vs. father-son relationship
- the importance of the response of others

There are very few accounts of fathers as education practitioners – whether teachers, teaching assistants, educational psychologists, advisors and so on. This seems rather odd, given that many of the role functions of parents seem to overlap those traditionally seen as the province of teachers – early educator, promoter of pro-social behaviours, and arbiter in cases of disputes between children and so on. *Every Child Matters* (2003) the English government's agenda for children and youth, presents a menu of responsibilities which could easily stand as a script for fatherhood. It identifies five themes with which parents of all children would doubtless identify in seeking to ensure the welfare of their sons: being healthy, staying safe, enjoying and achieving, make a positive contribution and achieving economic well-being.

A number of writers have acknowledged the intersection between teacher's professional and private personae. Thus, Sikes (1985) refers to the stressors on teachers as they move beyond the first phase of their career and into a phase represented by parenthood and increasing professional responsibility. Teachers are now required to privately juggle the demands of the five themes in *Every Child Matters* with their own young family whilst encountering the same issues in their professional lives. This synthesis in operation suggests that there is a research opportunity lying in wait ...

In 2006 Day *et al* sought to explore the personal and professional identities of teachers. These authors note that the personal circumstances of teachers are important components and influences on their professional demeanour. Their large scale study, however, did not identify 'teacher-fathers' specifically; indeed, few studies make even passing mention of this group of professionals – even though there must be a good number of teachers who are at various stages of fatherhood. And what is somewhat surprising in this absence of coverage in the literature, highlighted in several of our narrative extracts, is that fathers who teach in the same setting as their sons learn are likely to encounter an additional stressor.

It is entirely possible that fathers who are also teachers distance themselves from their own children as part of their 'professional' demeanor. Little has been made of this complex notion in terms of research effort, and it might seem to be somewhat marginal. But interestingly, there is evidence of a community of teacher-fathers who recognise this distancing strategy. One recent example is the comment of a discussant to an e-forum regarding the role of fathers in improving education: 'One knotty issue this debate doesn't seem to have covered is that of the parents who are teachers. My father was a teacher for around 20 years – certainly all of my secondary school years. For this very reason, we avoided any helping with homework for obvious reasons. At the end of the day, the teachers, teaching assistants and support staff in school are the ones trained to do this' (*BBC News*, 2005).

Another aspect of such distancing is the reluctance displayed by some prospective male teachers to move into primary school teaching or work in early-years settings (Sanders, 2002; Cunningham and Dorsey, 2004). On the other hand, the continuing negative impact of this might be reduced because of a growing tendency for men from middle-band social strata to express a preference for greater involvement in their son's child care and education (Wardle, 2004).

Some considerations for practitioners

Observations about the practical ramifications of being a teacher whilst also being a Dad are mainly anecdotal. Such is the paucity of research material regarding this topic that one has to utilise the informal views of individual teachers. Most educational settings certainly have informal rules about 'teacher professionalism', which will provide some framework for situations arising where a teacher comes in direct contact with his son. But it is difficult to account for the emotional response of fathers in such situations. What follows is an attempt to capture some of these feelings, using the words of one of the fathers who has participated elsewhere in this book, and who is also a classroom teacher.

Gerry is in his fifth year teaching in a primary school in the East Midlands of England. He had been following an award-bearing professional development programme at a local university, and consequently became known to one of the authors. We invited him to provide a brief written account of his dual role: Gerry had a son, Alfie, in Year 2 of the school in which he taught. When Alfie moves up to Year 3 in the next academic year (2008-9) he will most likely be taught by his father.

Gerry indicated that he seldom thought that he worked in the same school as his son: '*To me it's a job, and I want to do my very best at it. I have to be very professional, and I'm sure that whole days go by without my thinking in an educational sense about Alfie*'. Gerry told us: '*... whatever else happens, whatever emotions come into play, you have to leave aside the 'father' bit. I think I'd let Alf down if I did anything different*'. So there are definite notions of both recognition of the father-son relationship, whilst at the same time an almost compensatory over-statement about a reified professional position. Gerry states that '*I come across Alfie of course during lunchtimes and playtimes. There's never been a problem. I think, like me, he tries to avoid bringing attention to the fact that he's my lad ... maybe he thinks even now that it's not all that cool, I don't know.*'

These views are those of a teacher whose role does not bring him directly into contact with his son at the moment. Gerry's standpoint regarding his father-teacher/son relationship appears to be less straightforward. He expresses some uncertainty about his own emotional response to being in closer educational contact with Alfie: '*I really don't know how things will work out. I'm not all that worried at present, although I do admit that I sometimes wonder how I'll react ... for instance, if I see other children bullying him or isolating him because he's my son. I suppose I'm just trying to get to grips with how I'd react in that situation ... when it's much closer to home*'.

There is undoubtedly a fruitful area for thematic enquiry here: teachers' lives have prompted numerous research studies, both small-scale and national in profile. But we still have little which sheds light on the emotional, social and professional dimensions of fathers who, as teachers, professionally interact with their sons. Moreover, there is probably even less on the ways that these within-school relationships are played out within family settings.

8

Fathers as classroom helpers

I love being with the kids. Having them close to me makes me feel that I have a purpose other than just going home at night, barrowing the food through the front door, hunter-gatherer style. I've usually got a sense of wariness leading to distance with the boy and of course that's natural. I make myself think like a teacher, very professional and sometimes that's tough on me and it's not great for him either. You're emotion-free. And that's sad for me because all children need emotion. What makes things even worse is that I feel myself – and it is almost a wilfully physical thing – withdrawing from even slight emotional connection with my lad. Yet I think I'll give lots more to other kids in the class. Sometimes I am left wondering whether this is correct. Whether it is ethical. Well, is it? Should a dad be standing back and watching his lad do this or that and feel that he can't be involved? I wouldn't – don't – do it in the house and I shouldn't do it in work. But I conform to a lot of expectations [B]

A major problem as a father in school is that I'm treated with a lot of reservation by most of the teachers. They see it as if I've got the best of both worlds. And I think some parents see it a bit like that too. It's like 'He's on the inside, he's got the advantage'. I'm supposed to be able to use a position of privilege to gain more of whatever it is ... teacher-time, resources, influence, whatever – for my own child. People don't realise the balancing act. It's a bit similar to a teacher-referee in a school football match: the teacher from school A will give decisions against his own school more easily because he doesn't want to feel as though he's being biased towards his own place. I've never asked Seth how he feels for fear of drawing it to his attention. But I'm more likely than not to avoid contact, which is hard to do as we're both in the same classroom for a few lessons each day [B]

I was asked by his teacher whether I'd help out for a few hours in the school. Well, he'd probably have known ... well ... suspected that I wasn't working at the time ... he saw me there every day, bringing the kids in, standing there, talking with the others and not rushing off. I wasn't keen, to be honest. Felt a bit patronised if the truth be told ... you know, let's get the consolation Dad in to show we're trying to do things a bit different. I was a token Dad, a sort of badge for them and I wasn't happy with that, though I didn't tell them anything of the kind ... So I didn't do it. I've a new job now and so its not on anymore. But funnily enough, if they asked me again, now, in my position, I think I'd say 'Yes, sure I'll help out' ... I think that'd be good for my kids but I think the school needs it too because there's not enough men around the place [B]

We get loads of people. Random ... all sorts, coming in, doing this or that ... usually it's like ... women teachers ... no, not that ... you know, helping out and all that ... helping in the classroom ... but it was, it was women teachers, but then, they were all women in our school. We had one kid , eh, eh ... he was funny and a bit well, you could say he was funny ... you know, up there and stuff like that. We'd called him MandM ... do you understand? Shit, good eh ... .and ... .you know MandM because he was OK, quite hard really ... on the outside, but he was nuts in the middle ... his brain and ... But he had ... one day, this guy walks in ... he was big and he sits with M and they have a talk, big thing and I'm looking at it and Weeksy is as well. It turns out he's his Dad and that he's in school to help him, give him some backup. And ... well ... Actually, that was good, sound, his Dad turning up like that. It took balls, fair play ... [C]

He came into the school a few times and I was doing GCSEs so I had a lot of free time. I'd go and try and find him ... big my self up because my Dad was the man who was in to sort out the network, that sort of thing ... embarrassing now, really. The teachers knew too, and I think they all must have laughed at me, this kid who was trying to be ... trying to be cool, the big guy. My Dad didn't think much of it neither and he was glad to get away I think ... I didn't think it then but now I think I must have come across as a right Daddy's boy [C]

Themes highlighted by these fathers and sons in their narratives:

- fathers are positive about helping in class
- fathers frequently feel like outsiders in the classroom
- their involvement as helpers is positively recognised by other boys
- evidence of fathers feeling uncertain about their role in the classroom

It is probably accurate to state that men and schools have a tenuous relationship for the most part. Traditionally the mother has been the person most inclined to be responsible for school matters – whether taking and collecting children from school, especially at primary level, dealing with social arrangements such as sleepovers, lunch arrangements and so on and with oversight of school progress, including completing homework and responding to school correspondence. Such a role position requires mothers to come into early and reasonably frequent face-to-face contact with schools: they consequently become familiar with its territory and its protocols.

So it is understandable that much of the literature relating to fathers in schools contains references to their marginalisation (DfES, 2004). Yet successful involvement of fathers – including their role as classroom helper – has been identified as a major contributor to improved academic performance (Feinstein and Symons, 1999), better behaviour (Razwan, 2000), less criminality (Goldman, 2004), improvements in mental health outcomes and more successful adult relationships (Hobcraft, 1998).

The literature about the active involvement of fathers in schools is growing steadily. And it consistently amplifies the important performance linkages we have just indicated. The significance of promoting the involvement of fathers in classrooms is also linked to the low numbers of male primary school teachers in England, and a correspondingly low number of male teaching assistants.

As with other aspects of father-involvement in their son's education, the issue of professional attitudes has been highlighted as an inhibiting factor. Thus, McBride and Rane (2001) and McBride, Rane and Bae (2000) have highlighted the need to work with the professional community of the school in developing positive attitudes towards the involvement of fathers in classrooms. With regard to boys who are deemed to be at risk of educational or social failure, an evaluation study by Fagan and Iglesias (1999) was conducted to examine the effects of participation in a *Head Start*-based father involvement intervention programme for fathers and their children. The results suggest a positive association between higher levels of father involvement and the improvement of learning and behaviour of their sons.

Some considerations for practitioners

All the evidence that has accrued from academic research and large-scale evaluation studies, as well as that emerging in countless small-scale case-studies, suggests that the involvement of fathers in schools and classrooms is nearly always beneficial. In sum, the findings suggest that gains are to be had in boys' academic performance and their social behaviour too. A father will tend to be emotionally closer to his son as he progresses through his teenage years, and there is a strong correlation in the sense of positive well-being and happiness in the child. Closer involvement affords fathers pay-offs too. They have an opportunity to re-enter the world of children, and this elicits a whole range of things to talk about with the child. It is also good for the emotional balance and well-being of fathers themselves: most Dads want to be more involved in their son's schooling than their own father was. And there is increasing evidence that many boys themselves want their fathers to be more involved in their learning.

It is sometimes difficult for fathers to be fully involved with their son's education because they are unfamiliar with the way that schools function. Fathers frequently comment, for instance, on the fact that the school gates are surrounded by mums; they also say that schools, especially primary schools, don't have many male teachers. Furthermore, most communication with the home is addressed to the mother.

At the outset, therefore, schools need to recognise that if they wish to create male-friendly schools, certain things need to be done to make sure that such impressions (although true) are counteracted by other more father-orientated messages. Amongst the strategies that primary and secondary schools can adopt are:

- opening lines of communication directly with fathers
- actively seeking out input to school activities by fathers whether as classroom helpers, assisting on school journeys, participating in school sports and social activities
- publicising mentoring and coaching roles which provide opportunity for fathers to present pro-education models
- promoting social-coaching roles for fathers during break or lunchtimes
- positively discriminating in the appointment of men as teaching assistants
- inviting fathers to present at assemblies and other school gatherings
- providing regular opportunities for fathers particularly to come into their son's classroom at the start of the school day
- holding fathers-only events such as a Father's Day in school
- including a explicit statement valuing the involvement of fathers within the school's handbook
- arranging coaching and mentoring sessions for fathers about boys' learning

In all of this it is important that schools recognise that because of deep-seated beliefs, misconceptions or experiences, attitudinal change will inevitably be slow. And fathers themselves can do a number of straightforward things to enable a shift to take place. Some of the simple measures that can be considered are:

- for primary Dads, picking your son up from school whenever possible
- ensure that when you take your son into school in the morning you leave enough time to go into the classroom and look at the work he is doing

- familiarise yourself with the school handbook and its policies
- get to know your son's teachers so that you can talk about a teacher by name to your son
- offer to provide a demonstration or assembly input if you have a special skill or interest
- make sure you read notes, letters, newsletters and other communications from the school
- listen to your son read on a regular basis!
- celebrate your son's achievements – if he has a homework book, reading diary or achievement book, make sure you sign it as often as possible
- always find time to talk to your son – not necessarily about school
- share in some of your son's topic work or projects
- always speak positively about your own school experiences, even if you were often unhappy in school
- try to avoid being openly critical of your son's school in front of him. If you have concerns or if there is something you don't agree with, approach the school and seek a settlement.

9

Who needs them? Non-resident fathers

My Dad was in the Army, so we got used to him being away from home. When he was first posted I remember being very sad and crying a lot. I was five, I think, so not old. My Mum still hadn't had Sophie yet, so it was just me and her. I could see she was sad as well, and that made it worse. When he came back the first time, he was in the first Iraq thing, it was like a big Christmas event, it was incredible, really incredible. My Mum was crying and he was close to it ... he'd never seen Sophie, never before ... and I remember him turning, looking down at me and feeling these big, brown hands, strong hands, lifting me up off the floor, high up over everybody ... I could see the soldiers, still coming off the plane and other people kissing ... And he dropped me onto his chest and he smelled of sweat, sweet sweat and I just cried out 'Dad! Will you play football with me?' I'll never forget it [A]

He was there and he wasn't. My Dad was in and out. Getting him to say he'd 'be there' was dead easy. Getting him there was different. Mum was let down so many times. I'd feel like crying for her because she put on all sorts ... she'd mask it all, put on a show, like she was in Hollywood ... great, except, no ... not for her, it wasn't great at all. But that was how he was. All sorts of good intentions, all sorts of well, you know ... eh ... 'I'll do this, that ... eh ... I'll be there'. And the 'son'. The fucking son. And he was never there ... not for her, not for me ... and still, it was 'son'. And, fuck me, I resent ... shit, how I resent him not doing that, not having any honesty to do it ... be there, and yet coming in with 'son', as though I was his, just because of something, some connection, biological ... Well, angry, yes you can see, I am fucking angry ... I'm sorry, but it's nothing to do with you ... him ... he's not helped me. Oh, shit, no ... I'd like to do him, do him because he did it all to us all ... Mum, Marti (sister), all of us. All this being there, son shit. I'll be a Dad and fuck me ... I'd better be different [A]

When I spend time away from home I always fret. I wonder who'll polish the school-shoes that need to be polished to show the world I care. I devise elaborate plans to disguise my not being there [B]

We split up when he was 7. I had to go. There was nothing going on, like ... nothing ... no-one else. It was just finished and we'd both known it for ages. You battle with it, fight it but soon you're fighting yourselves and then you reach the point where you're saying 'Stop!' It was a tough time, a bad time for us, all of us. It'd been better I think if there'd been somebody else, on either side because then you'd have something to blame it on. But as it happened, there wasn't anything. The kids both cried. They got upset every time I was at the house and then she asked me not to keep calling because it was getting to them too much. He (son) was bad, very bad sometimes and she (ex-wife) said that he was crying at school and getting into bother. Those were the earliest memories for me. I'm glad for me that we split, but I feel guilt that I wasn't there for Robert (son) when I needed to be. That's a Dad, isn't it? [B]

We stay with my Dad every two weeks for the whole weekend. We have fun. He makes us laugh. He's a lot different than he was with my Mum, and that's good because they don't have rows anymore. I'm happy because he's close by now ... before he lived far away, across the other side ... out in Fenton and we'd miss seeing him. I like it when he comes to get us from school and we come running out to him. And I feel happy because he's alright now with my Mum as well. He's kinder and that makes me feel safer [C]

I'm OK about him being not here anymore. I'm happy, because he wasn't good for us. He did stuff, thieving, drugs ... nothing heavy, with violence or that but ... we got a bad reputation, our family, because of him. We'd get in trouble at school because he'd been up there a few times shouting ... he was drunk and it wasn't good ... Yes, I'm pleased he's not around no more [C]

Themes highlighted by these fathers and sons in their narratives:

- remembering critical relationship events
- inconsistent fathering
- negative role models
- trying to be a 'dad from a distance'
- re-defining father-son relationships after family breakdown
- surviving abusive fathering

A non-resident father – sometimes inaccurately referred as an 'absent father' – is a parent who does not live in the same household as his son. There could be many reasons for this: divorce or separation, working away for extended periods or, increasingly frequently, an inability to formally commit to a relationship after the conception or birth of their son. There is also great variety in the level of contact between non-resident fathers and their sons, and in the quality of their interactions. Since evidence shows that sons who feel close to their fathers are statistically more resilient to adolescent risk activity, including drug-related behaviours (Furstenberg and Harris, 1993), emotional bonding between father and son appears to be crucial in inhibiting problematic behaviour.

There has been much research on the relationship between mother and son, with Bowlby (1951) pre-eminent in the field. He stressed the centrality of the mother's role: 'an infant and and young child should experience a warm, intimate and continuous relationship with his (*sic*) mother (or permanent mother figure) in which both find satisfaction and enjoyment'. Whilst few would argue, Bowlby extended the degree and intensity of emotional attachment with the mother to develop his theory of maternal deprivation. He maintained that maternal deprivation would be likely to cause serious negative and largely irreversible effects on the child's intellectual, social and emotional development.

In 1989 Hodges and Tizard powerfully challenged Bowlby's position, maintaining that even if a child did not have a mother figure she or he could still form attachments with other adults. Certainly, evidence now obtaining has done much to render Bowlby's stance to be incapable of generalisation.

Non-resident or 'absent' fathers have always been newsworthy. There is something which strikes chords punctuated by an admix of prurience and a British sense of 'decency': the social 'crime' of deserting the family ranks high in the premiership of male shortcomings. And where public opinion is likely to be manifest by tut-tut, told-you-so, head-shaking disapproval or downright antagonism, so there will be politicians riding towards the already rotting carcass of family life. The line goes that absent fathers are the cause of delinquency, poor levels of school attainment amongst boys, and girls for that matter, and for what is regularly constructed as a juvenile malaise of excess, impropriety and fecundity. Absent or non-resident fathers might yet end up being blamed for all the world's problems.

Part of the social taboo which surrounds the non-resident father is borne out of a historical version of what being a father came to mean. 'Our Father' carries huge emotional and social symbolism across many cultures and groups. A public acceptance, scarcely understanding, of His omnipotent power and knowledge was in many cases translated, as if by alchemy, into a God(father) of the family, whose role-performance could career from strict moral authoritarianism to nurturing, caring figurehead. And every other emotional, social and economic function could be haphazardly visited. Yet there is considerable evidence to support a contrasting view, namely that many non-resident fathers have strong bonds with their sons and families (McLanahan and Booth, 1989).

Smoke without fire? Well, there is some degree of homespun truth in such deterministic and pejorative opinion. Thus, Coley and Medeiros (2007) confirm earlier research evidence – which is substantial and mainly equivocal – that the lack of a father figure does have a significant negative effect. Their own study comprised a large sample of teenagers (647) from 'poor urban families' where the father was not resident. Coley and Medeiros illustrate the 'protective' function of fathers with regard to teenage male 'at-risk' factors. We should, nonetheless, be cautious in assuming a single-factor explanation for the difficulties experienced and the challenges posed by boys whose father is, for whatever reason, absent from the home.

Elsewhere in this book we note the importance placed on the involvement of fathers in their son's education. Across a range of other social indicators, boys thrive when there is evidence of active involvement by fathers (Nord, Brimhall and West, 1997) and so there is at the very least a pragmatic value in making greater efforts to include non-resident fathers more centrally in their son's schooling.

Some considerations for practitioners

It is vital that schools take account of the shift away from conventional family units. One in seven families now contain a stepfather, and there is an increasing number of families who have no permanent adult male in the household. Patterns of parenting are therefore becoming far more non-standard and varied, and schools need to acknowledge this in the way that they operate. This is especially important since many of the most vulnerable boys will be from such families.

Schools need to recognise the scale of the phenomenon as a whole and be aware, through pastoral arrangements, of just who the pupils are. At the same time it is essential that no stereotypical assumptions are made: non-resident fathers do not always cause difficulties within the remaining family unit. But it is nonetheless important to plan for situations which might cause embarrassment or misunderstanding – or worse. Certain things need to be borne in mind by the school in doing this, including:

- ensuring that an opportunity is made to define explicitly how lines of communication will work in practical terms
- recognising that fathers prefer direct contact by telephone, text or e-mail to communication via their son
- recognising, and building in, appropriate child-protection procedures where necessary
- recognising that both parents have a right to all the information about a pupil – being absent from the home does not interfere with this, unless there are issues surrounding child or parent safety

- incorporating an understanding that there may be negative effects on a boy's learning and behaviour in school if his father is no longer resident in the home.

There are also pointers for fathers themselves. Family separation often causes personal trauma and extreme emotions, both internalised and acted-out. A metaphor illustrating this process is the joint bank account, in which both father and son deposit and withdraw emotion and feelings of self-actualisation. As the adult participant the father has the major responsibility in ensuring that the account is maintained in credit. A withdrawal is made each time the son witnesses a trauma associated with separation, divorce or other family upheaval. If there is no counterbalancing deposit, for example in being able to talk to the boy in non-judgemental terms about exactly what is going on, then he will be increasingly less likely to contribute to the account in the future. The long-term impact would be that the account becomes bankrupt and there would be a serious risk that the father-son relationship would be foreclosed.

Similar considerations apply to dealing with schools and other educational settings. Schools are, for the most part, child-centred places where the best interests of the pupils are at the heart of everything that goes on. They are also mainly places which are adaptable. But they can only function effectively in supporting pupils who are experiencing a domestic crisis of whatever form if they are given relevant information so that they can put in place a workable plan to support the pupil. In our experience, the real facts relating to a father's absence come only after the emotional impact of separation has been manifest by the boy's deteriorating learning and behaviour. Many schools now have sophisticated frameworks for the transfer of sensitive information between staff and fully recognise the importance of confidentiality and trust. These mechanisms are vital for the establishment of a culture of positive engagement with non-resident fathers.

10

Dealing with difficulties: SEN and disability

He was called Desmond. His father had the same name. Poor little waif, fragile, timid, big eyes that looked permanently bewildered. No wonder. She told me, Annie, his wife, yes, I think wife, that her husband peed the bed every night, Broke down right there in the nursery when I gave her 50p to get the bus to Darnall to see her social worker. I wanted to comfort her but the smell of stale piss on her made me retch and seek the breeze from the open window ... He used to hit little Desmond, who never knew what quite he had done. Home from the pub, complain about the 'crap' meal Annie had scraped together from the child benefit she'd managed to keep back when he raided her purse for beer money. Then, drunk, he'd go to their bed, and either too lazy or unconscious he would pee. They had no washing machine, no money for the launderette so Annie told me she did her best in the sink. I offered her the use of the nursery washing machine. She said she'd be too embarrassed 'the sheets aren't nice', she said ... [A]

I remember William only too well. He was the boy in the jumper, all purple and festooned with wool-balls, badges to his abiding poverty – a poverty that was to become him through performances, goals and outcomes. I recall lying in bed in those stark hours between awareness and mystery, between the fear of sleep and the refuge of night, hearing voices straining up stairways to alarm my senses. It was, for me – and I suppose William – a time of approaching separation, a parting of the ways and of more monumental sadnesses at life's frail dusting of advantage. I cried those little-boy big-tears that 11 year-olds should never cry, my head resting on the salted bolster as I willed for the sleep that would save me. What was to become of him, this William, carbon-drill eyes gazing into distant yet predictable futures, all Halsey on legs and diminishing as I even thought the very thought. Laid bare I came to regard these things as the machinery of indulgence and self-congratulation. They were not about William – how could they be in a mind so ill-prepared for reflection, still less for charity? Those genuflections speak more of who I am than anything about the boy in the jumper. My bowed state was a Marshall Plan for approbation and relief, much less so for the promotion of real changes in and for who I was at that captured moment – and whosoever I'd become in my summers and autumns. For, in the morning, it would be light in my head and I could return to a rounder, less complicated world. A world that William never knew, or would scarcely have the keys to enter.

And I did think, and kept thinking then and now, about who he, William was. I imagined, with effortless superiority that was now increasingly decorating a boy's version of how his world would be, a dim place where green paint badged the aspiration and washing on Monday-lines signalled a will to toe the line. He'd have a Dad himself of course, working in all probability those long hours before the sun poured down Eddleston Road to move the suits and ties to more sensible work. That man would have big hands, far bigger than those of my own father. And they'd announce the brutal and surely dangerous work they did by red, raised flesh here, or an elastoplast trophy there, framed by fingernails which were more often black. And the routine Woodbine yellow would tell me that he smoked, as even William did: even then a sign of both manhood bursting to get out and of an acceptance that he too would inherit his Dad's life on the railway and its social net. He'd no doubt too would ensure his own son learned to wear his work as clothes of honour [B]

I'm out of my depth ... I want so much to help but I'm lost really. Put it like this. When I went to school there were bright 'uns and thick buggers. Bet you can guess which one was me ... there was no arguments, no questions. The teachers told us and we knew it anyway. All this calling us in to discuss this and that. It's not fooling anyone really. I mean. I'm not daft and between you me and that door we know ... well, you must know in your position. It's what goes on ... but dressing it up as some kind of divine right to have summat to say. I'd rather them tell me that Troy's thick, like they used to. I got on OK because nowt was expected of me and yet they did a right good job on getting me into college. I mean, these days they'd be sat there, scratching their heads and wondering how they could get me to a university. I think they expect that of him (Troy) too ... and that's stupid, daft ... we know him, I go fishing with him, talk to him. He wants to follow me into this line of work, that's what's best for him ... but they'll not do much for him to get him there. I left school before I was 16 and I dare-say that's when he should leave too [B]

Dad wasn't really 'there' ... do you know ... he wasn't connected with what was going on with me at all. And ... well ... he was scared I'd say. Really scared, because he'd ... not done ... got on well in school. Schools were like ... it makes me laugh, it is a really stupid, stupid connection to make but ... he said that being in (my) school was like being in Armani, the store, shop, you know ... he was ... well, a bit fat but not much, not all that much but. It's just that he'd not fit in there. He'd look like a perv ... no, not that ... outside of it, all those clothes. But then there was what he thought and ... he really did think that these things, clothes and stuff like that ... weren't ... didn't belong to him. Oh, just out of his league, too up-market and all that ... all that about not being good enough. And yes, he'd ... he saw the school just like that, he was, well, not worthy ... out of ... it was just that the school was something different, not part of him ... frightened him. He wasn't part of it. Yes, sad, sad and ... he was never made to be-long. They should have done that, at least they should ... [C]

My Dad is good to me. He plays with me. He is the best Dad. He has red hair. My Dad has a Ford. He can drive it fast. He makes me laugh. He loves my Mum [C]

Themes highlighted by these fathers and sons in their narratives:

- emotional attachments: surrogate fathering or 'thinking like a father'
- key individuals and events inform responses
- helplessness and frustrations
- reluctance to be involved based on personal fears and histories
- actualised sons

The prospect of caring for a newly arrived son, or daughter, is a daunting prospect for many fathers. Levels of expectation are imposed, then raised and further imposed. There are rules, protocols of intimate family and wider culture, to be followed. Amidst it all there is a constant and rhythmic backdrop commentary by others on the decisions and departures that fathers visit on their sons. The Les Dawson mother-in-law caricature is borrowed with surprising ease, because those older, more informed 'others' know best.

But what happens when men encounter an arguably greater challenge in their role as father? The arrival of an infant who has a disability, or the gradual recognition that a growing child has a learning difficulty or emergent disability, is a major trauma for most parents. This is especially the case when there has been little or no indication that it might happen. The literature is replete with references to the responses of parents as a couple to the task of parenting a disabled child (Cox and Lambrenos, 1992; Hadadian, 1995; Howe, 2005; Hassall and Rose, 2005). But, as with the case with the generic literature on 'parents' and 'families', the role of the father is often hardly touched upon in these studies. (Gavidia-Payne and Stoneman, 2004). Indeed, McConkey (1994) refers to fathers, in the context of families with a disabled child, as being 'hard to reach'.

Some studies have attempted to establish the ways in which fathers respond, rationalise and function when their child has a disability. Amongst the earliest were those by Vadasy *et al* (1985) and Meyer (1986), both of which documented the benefits of an increased involvement by men. They reveal that the reactions of fathers and mothers have certain similarities. For instance, both parents have to address feelings of grief when finding out that their child has a disability, and then to deal with new and different responsibilities as carers and nurturers. Meyer (1986) points out one difference however: whereas fathers tended to look at the future prospects for their disabled child, mothers were inclined to be more preoccupied and stressed by the day-to-day concerns.

In an exploration of fathers' involvement in the Head Start programmes in the USA, researchers based at the *National Center on Fathers and Families* at the University of Pennsylvania found that fathers were more likely to be involved in these initiatives if they had a son in the programme than a daughter (NCOFF, 1999). Although the study does not indicate how many children had been ascertained as having a disability or learning difficulty, such data help policy-makers to draw some conclusions as to patterns of male-involvement in early-intervention programmes.

Another early study relating to fathers was conducted by League and Ford (1996). They provide a useful summary of the benefits of fathers' involvement in education generally but complement this with an overview of the research relating to their involvement in schooling when their child had a learning difficulty or disability. As with other studies in this area (see, for example, Carpenter and Herbert, 1997) data-generalisability is something of an issue, because sample sizes are understandably small. But League and Ford do offer some useful insights into the role of fathers in this context, whilst noting that the potential for their involvement has not been fully realised.

Carpenter and Herbert (1997) have explored the role played by fathers from the perspective of their own needs as fathers. The impetus for their work bears testimony to the relatively sparse nature of research and development in the area of fathers and their disabled children. During a literature mapping exercise referring to the arrival of a newborn child with a disability they note that '... an increasing awareness developed about how little was known about the reactions of fathers in these circumstances'. The accounts they provide describe feelings of anger, numbness and shock. These fathers were also very suspicious of the educational professionals they came in contact with. They felt unable to express feelings of grief because they had to appear strong and competent in the face of a family 'crisis'. And they considered themselves to be 'different' from other parents, being especially watchful of their body-language.

These feelings are being experienced at the time when the father, like the mother and the disabled child himself, are at their most vulnerable. The needs of the father often go unnoticed by professionals (*Social Care Institute for Excellence*, 2005). This is hardly surprising when they are seen as 'the invisible parent' (Ballard, 1994) or 'just a shadow' (West, 2000).

Many of these responses have been confirmed in the generic literature relating to parents of disabled children. There is a rich collection of historical accounts about how parents of disabled children were viewed by society at large (Sandow and Garner, 1994). The medieval preoccupation with magic and the idea of a 'visitation of handicap' as punishment for moral lapses is very much to the fore. And there is long-standing acknowledgement that the parents of disabled children suffer feelings of guilt and failure. The literature on these themes is covered elsewhere (see, for example, Minnes, 1998).

Rogers (2007) highlights the wide range of responses from parents who have a child with learning disability, and these can be inferred as relating as much to fathers as to mothers. We have already pointed to the trauma experienced by parents when discovering that their child is somehow 'different', and to feelings of disappointment and what Rogers refers to as 'dashed expectations'. She quotes one father to illustrate this. 'Tim' tells her: 'It's dreadful really ... I think it's like ... possibly when you hear of someone who's died suddenly in a family say, as opposed to an older person. And you really can't believe it ... one of the parts of the shock is that you really can't believe it ... well perhaps I'll wake up tomorrow and it won't be there, and of course as it goes on and you realise that it will be there and that's part of the shock' (p.138).

The response of denial has been well documented, both the short-term response to the trauma of finding out or, as sometimes happens when the special need relates to underachievement or emotional and behavioural difficulties, a more elongated form of explaining – or even justifying – difference. Using denial in this way is a common human response, and it functions as a means of protecting or insulating parents from the reality they might otherwise face (Seligman and Darling, 1997).

Some parents will meet any suggestion that their child has a learning difficulty with anger, hostility and even externalised aggression, especially when it is an educational or other professional who is raising concern. This is particularly true in the case of 'emotional and behavioural difficulties'. Roffey (2002) illustrates this with the responses of some the parents in her study although, as usual in this literature, she does not mention fathers *per se*.

The literature on fathers and disability or learning difficulties tends to steer a wide berth round explorations of the views of fathers of boys who are deemed to have an 'emotional or behavioural difficulty'. Or it could be that this group of fathers – within which non-resident fathers are significantly over-represented – are the hardest of the 'hard to reach' in terms of both practical action and researching them (Bridges, 1987).

One aspect of the literature that has been particularly influential and certainly relevant to practice is the variations in parent-child interaction and subsequent levels of attachment. It is widely accepted that the degree to which parents handle stressors in child-rearing will strongly influence the formation of attachments between them and their child (Susman-Stillman *et al,* 1996). What these and other studies demonstrate is the extent to which the levels and quality of attachment vary according to the type of disability experienced by the child (Howe, 2006). Thus, Barnett *et al* (1999) showed that amongst a sample population of children with Down's syndrome, autism, cerebral palsy, cleft palate and congenital heart disease, the children who had the severest disabilities formed the strongest attachments. In part this is explained by the fact that an increased 'visibility', either in physical terms or demonstrated by medical diagnosis, enhances parents' recognition and acceptance. We are reminded of the words of one of our father-respondents, whose son had a congenital abnormality, who said that '... the lad is nothing to anybody but me. I will care for him, I'll make sure he's safe ... *I* will'.

Some considerations for practitioners

Like research on the involvement of fathers in their sons' education, the case of their responses to SEN and disability issues has tended to be subsumed under the generic header of 'parents'. This applies both in the academic literature and with regard to documents offering practical advice.

Following the admonition by League and Ford in 1996 that much more needed to be done to ensure greater involvement of fathers in their child's special education programme, there has been some development in this area. There are a number of practical steps that schools can take. Many special settings are already well versed in these approaches, although mainstream schools are less likely to be conversant with them or to adopt them in practice.

One obvious issue, and one which distinguishes the experiences of fathers of children who have SEN or a disability, is their emotional response to unexpected circumstances. Very often the father's own emotional needs, including a need for support, can go unrecognised. Schools can, therefore, alert the parent, via the special educational needs coordinator (SENCO), to the existence of various sources of information, advice and support.

Procedures in special education are heavily underpinned by statutory documentation and by abundant school-related assessment or monitoring materials and schools need to ensure that these are made easily accessible to fathers. Review meetings and other events concerning the educational progress of the (learning) disabled boy need to take account of the father's work pattern.

As with bereavement, men tend to mask their emotions and remain externally stoical in the face of the potential trauma, emotional stress or practical challenges presented by their son being disabled or having learning difficulties. Schools can be hugely proactive in promoting positive relationships with the fathers. Many special schools, for example, have taken forward plans to introduce dedicated training opportunities for fathers (see, for example, Carpenter *et al*, 2004) in which training topics are directly related to their needs. Moreover, such training is designed to maximise engagement with fathers, using active-learning, problem-solving and other male-orientated learning strategies.

The advent of 'extended schools' in England (DfES, 2002) has done much to promote flexible working, so that fathers can more easily access the educational services they provide at times which are sympathetic to their employment patterns. Whilst this issue is of generic importance in education, there can be little doubt that such changes in the way schools are organised will enable greater access by fathers who have sons who have learning difficulties.

Many of these initiatives have been largely built around the expertise of special settings and their tradition of working closely with parents and advocates, is of enormous importance to fathers generally. They offer models of effective practice which can be generalised beyond special schools and can help fathers to be resilient and engage with the educational challenges facing their sons. And many of these initiatives require few specialist resources and can be grown in and from existing clusters of schools, centred around special settings.

11

Tyrants on the touchline: Fathers and sport

Dad was gentle in spite of his moods which even beyond the grave could waft over the house like the grey rolling cloud down over Kinder Scout and on and on. I played football and never heard him call, never felt his vein-bulging, pop-eyed head on a stick roaring frustration that were some other fathers' visitations on their sons. Even in an Old Trafford bulging to capacity my Dad would be subdued in silence, without judgement or rancour at our team's failure to win. One time, in those make-believe days of schoolboy wonder, with United moving towards one holy grail, we stood in mute suffocation as our team, The Team, expired on our dream. The exit from Europe was inglorious, more so on account of the pit-bull brawl that punctuated the legitimate action. Horizontal in the Manchester mud, our Red lad – not known as a doormat – ensured that at least those Belgrade communists left with a mark, if not a goal against them. All around us the sea of angry red cheered him as he struck the pyrrhic blows. All around us too was encouragement to leave our silent watching and join the corporate animosity. At the point of crescendo my brother was visited by his demons, spectacularly so in the context of our father-and-sons relationship. His throwaway, mood-dictated but scarcely insulting, heat-seeking word missile was launched from the screaming paddock. It was to be ordnance that never found its target, deflected by Dad's silent look of betrayal, embarrassment and, ultimately, anger. There would be no more Reds, no more men and boys together. If we couldn't 'behave yourself' and couldn't show that we'd been 'brought up' not to sink to the lowest 'common (as muck)' denominator of all – the use of language unbecoming – then we were told, on that uncompromising drive back down Cheshire lanes, that we'd never visit the promised land again. And my brother's word? It was 'hound' – yes, utter blasphemy, verbal aggression verging on audio-porn, all rolled into that single frustrated call of a defeated 12-year old United fundamentalist. Hound! It seems unreal to think of the word in terms of the level of threatened retribution it had then provoked [A]

But the story spills over, as it illustrates the Dad on repeated touchlines – Crewe, Stoke-on-Trent and the length and breadth of Wales – as his growing son articulated his hopelessness on the killing fields. Amid the mundane performances, surfaced by a never-say-die (even on those killing fields), run until you evaporate, compensation that at least I'd learnt from him, I was conscious of his quiet study of my efforts. No room, then, for the brutal, instep-crushing challenges that were my trademark in those games when my living and breathing conscience was absent. It was an understated dignity. I don't think he ever 'shouted' as such, still less felt able to have me endure the ceaseless cajoling and chastising that seems to be a requirement for any Dad on the touchline. There'd be a few words of quiet encouragement and for those lines, said unprompted and with an almost tangible embarrassment, I felt grateful. Part of his encouragement was in making sure that my boots were clean. My other kit was sorted by Mum, but boots were his domain, the ties that bound us in so many ways [A]

Dunno why it is I get up-tight. They think I'm a right twat, shouting and bawling my head off at him. But he gets lots of love, he's the boy and he knows I don't really mean it. I mean, he wouldn't want me mincing along the touchline like a fairy would he? At least this way he knows I'm there for him, I support him. Fucking hell, I could be like some of them others. I think they just ponce off the team ... treat it as some Dad's club or summat, stiff upper lip ... all that fucking nonsense. We go to win, my lad and me. I give him a shout, wind him up because he needs me to do that, to get stuck in, be a man, yes ... [B]

I never stop wondering what's going through the minds of some of those men, prowling up and down with the red face and eyes like big white gobstoppers. There's always some kind of yellow stuff around the sides of their mouth and they've got a look of the devil about them. I'm sure that if I was a kid I'd be absolutely terrified. It is all very antagonistic and hostile during the game. What is equally surprising is that afterwards they're as nice as pie, and they don't seem to understand that the boys probably don't understand the change from nasty Dad to this really decent, social being. As I say, it's beyond me ... One thing that I do notice ... I suppose it's a personal theory of mine ... that a lot of the men on the touchline, those who seem to shout the loudest and come across as the most vociferous and ... even angry ... seem to be the ... well, not to draw back ... the fattest ... There are some really big, and I mean very overweight, blokes and they chunder on and on, as though they've been there and done it. What I think, and I said it was my theory, is that they've not been all that good at it ... football ... and are desperately living out another chance through their son. Sad isn't a word I'd use ... tragic, very, very tragic. And it's rage too, rage by them against all the stuff that they've attempted to handle as ham-fisted men, short on sensitivity, short on sensible emotion, and certainly, yes, certainly a lot short of connecting with their kids who were definitely out there yelling back at their Dads – 'Please stop shouting at me ... please' [B]

I think 'Oh shut it Dad, stop it' because it makes me feel bad. Really bad and it's ... well ... it's not cool. I get embarrassed to be ... the ... me with the Dad who's shouting and ... kicking off, getting really serious, really ... drastic and, well ... sad, that's how it comes over. That's how it is ... I like ... mmm ... I get on with him (Dad) but I'm feeling ... not very ... it's your Dad but it's sad and ... I'm sorry about it because you know him ... you'll know ... but I want to run away, over the pitch, away from it because it makes me feel: 'Dad, you're not like this normally, you're not this ... person'. That's what's in my head, up here. And it is, that's it. That's what it is. My Dad's somebody else, running up and down, shouting, screaming and ... oh [C]

We go to training and to the game. He talks to me about how I play. He doesn't shout much, but he talks with other Dads. The good thing is that he knows about football, so I listen to him. I suppose I must do. I support the same team as him. He gets annoyed when he sees other boys turning up, not trying, being silly ... he says you should try hard for the team. I think that is a good thing to do [C]

Themes highlighted by these fathers and sons in their narratives:

- fathers and expectations, standards
- differential manifestations of 'support' for sons
- the importance of 'being there'
- embarrassment and humiliation at 'being shouted at'
- school sport as an expression of masculinity
- school sport as an opportunity to make emotional connections

Few aspects in the schooling of boys evince more involvement and emotion amongst fathers than their son's participation in school sport. Whilst many fathers present as passive yet supportive figures, gently encouraging their sons as just one of a group of youngsters engaged in a recreational pursuit, others can be far more strident and sometimes overtly aggressive.

This is not a new phenomenon and thus cannot be attributed to an increasingly competitive sports culture. Our narrative extracts, which date back to the 1940s, exemplify the often over-wrought passions of some fathers whose desire for success spills into highly visible and audible support which is often not welcomed by their son, by other boys or their fathers who support or help organise school sporting events.

Examples of such excess are regrettably numerous in the contemporary media. The BBC children's website, CBBC, recently used an electronic forum to gauge the views of children about their parents' involvement in school sport. One 11 year old, acknowledging the thinly disguised competitive streak that exists in many fathers, stated that 'I think it is a good idea that parents are banned from school sports days ... My dad always takes part in the parents race and has to win – so embarrassing' (CBBC, 2007). Other electronic forums carry reports on parental excesses – usually by fathers. In the United States, for instance, the *Kidzworld* website reported that 'Three parents were arrested after a full-scale brawl between parents, coaches and fans at a youth soccer game in San Diego in 2001' (*Kidzworld*, 2007). And the same site contained a chilling reminder of how extreme the response of some fathers could be to sporting failure or lack of opportunity: 'In April 2005, the father of a Texas high school football player shot and wounded his son's football coach because he didn't think his son was getting enough playing time' (*ibid*).

The *Guardian* newspaper ran a headline on June 22, 2005) which read: 'Parents 'ruining school sports day'. It is reported that, according to one piece of research, for some fathers 'Winning is everything, even if it means foul play, aggressive behaviour and possible injury'. The article stated that 'traditional sports days of yesteryear were ... more genteel days where sports day amounted to pleasant sack, three-legged and egg and spoon races'. Such whimsical and uncompetitive approaches existed because its sole function was 'embarrassing your dad'. Nowadays some fathers appear to have an urgent competitive streak which, if not manifest during an annual trial of athleticism against other parents, may find its outlet in their behaviour on the touchline of the football or rugby pitch. Certainly, this is one theme that emerges from our indicative narratives. As the *Guardian* article continues '... some parents have a highly competitive attitude to life and are neurotic about their children succeeding at everything they attempt. It is spoiling the whole thing'.

Fathers and sons often have a mutual interest in sport. At an early age boys are fed images which become embedded in their consciousness, beginning with their father being the source of rough-and-tumble play and the willing participant in quasi-competitive trials of strength or endurance, however child-orientated and informally serious. The boy will also witness his father presenting himself as a sportsman, often in the company of other young fathers, in various culturally popular team sports: football, cricket, rugby and so on, as well as sports like athletics, tennis and golf. To this can be added the male bonding between father and son from watching sporting events together on television or in person. What is created is the iconic image of the 'connected' father and son, sharing a sporting experience in which some manifestation of competitiveness is inevitable.

Some considerations for practitioners

The involvement of fathers in school sporting activity can generate positive outcomes for all concerned. Schools can benefit from the enthusiasm of many men for sport, from their natural competitive streak and their practical inputs in training, match-day organisation and so on. Many schools actively encourage such involvement at a various levels and certain projects provide useful practical pointers.

- schools need to be explicit about their expectations of fathers, formulating this as part of a home-school agreement
- fathers should be involved in developing a code of conduct for attending or participating in sporting events in school
- periodic meetings should be arranged to allow fathers opportunities to discuss sport-related issues
- regular communication with the home is especially helpful if it is directed to fathers by name
- sport should be recognised as a part of the school curriculum in which fathers can find ways of connecting with their son's school experience

Fathers themselves need to foster pro-social attitudes when supporting their sons in school sports events. They need to be aware that they can present to their sons an explicit modelling of appropriate interactions, thus actively participating in the social education of their sons to become citizens. The manner in which fathers accommodate the disappointment of defeat or offer encouragement and congratulation is particularly important. Witnessing adults recognising the skills and achievements in others even when they are on the opposing team gives boys a powerful message. And the degree to which the same fairness is articulated in post-match conversations with their sons helps boys to develop their ability to understand the importance of accepting winning and losing as part of the process of growing into a man.

Many fathers recognise their tendency to become excitedly over-involved at times during a competitive sporting encounter. This is understandable. But if it is recognised as an example of unsatisfactory social modelling by the father it can also be used to promote discussion with their sons about inappropriate behaviour. Being reflective and self-critical about one's own behaviour helps fathers to give their sons greater understanding of their own response to success and to disappointment. And it provides another opportunity for father and son to connect, by offering boys an occasion to gain deeper insight into their Dad's persona.

12

Fathers and bereavement

When my Dad died it really was a black and venomous day. I don't think there is anything to compare. The screaming frustration, pain, total sense of desperation. As I write this down I'm in the car you know. He bought it for me, all silver and newly smelly, that kind of garage boudoir smell that you can now buy in tins from Halfords. And it had 'factory-filled radials', too. I was a novice driver, and in retrospect I have to thank those watchful motorists who gave me wide clearance on that sorrowful highway to the south. I can't really remember all that much. But I do know that I must have gone like a zephyr, nothing passed me on the way – 270 miles of sometimes crying and a dull hurt coursing through me. I really didn't think it was me in that car. How could it be. Christ! He was young. And scarcely had he reached 50 and that stupid, malevolent 'God' that I'd been told would see us all through, keep us safe and free from harm, had called his number out for immediate membership of that vastly overrated music hall in the sky [A]

I can look at it now and talk to you ... in the kind of cliché that they always use for deaths that are noble, adventurous and probably quite romantic if you're looking at it from a distance ... I do that myself ... you know, talking about him in a kind of mantra ... 'dying doing what he liked doing best ... he would have wanted to have gone this way ... It was quick, didn't feel a thing' ... all of those words that people say, and I've had them said to me. This might seem daft ... a bit ... scary really to you, but him dying like he did was ... well, I sometimes feel as though I was robbed of a chance to grieve, do all of that angry, screaming stuff that sons must do when they want to understand. But, strange ... because people saw his death as a sort of adventurous death, a sporting accident ... kind of was saying to me that I wasn't allowed to grieve too much, at least not out in the open [A]

Roger Fawcett, with Mr Fletcher stepped behind and grey as his suit, walked in to my high-jinx with the Year 8s. I muttered an embarrassed welcome, sheepishly ferreting for papers, texts or something to make me seem like a teacher worthy of the name. He looked without a smile. I was in trouble it seemed. Roger said 'I need a word, Mr Garner', the command of a friend professionalised by protocol.

Now my head was buzzing. I was – you will recall – elated by the day's earlier events. I could take admonition. I was cast-iron. I was a superhero.

'Roger is taking you home', said Mr Fletcher.

Those words rang and still ever ring in my mind. They creep along my subconscious corridors and – as I've subsequently come to recognise – have informed my responses to children and young people – even life – ever since.

I do recall that journey but can't fully remember its numbness or its meaning. All those years ago there was a motor car – two stroke I understand – called a Wartburg. It looked and sounded like its name. Manfully constructed, square and uncompromising in an East European sort of way, I imagined the workforce at Wartburg plc – what stories this dashboard, these clumsy switches and dials could all tell, could they speak. The slow streets of Coventry swept by (is that the right phrase – Wartburg remember). It was moving to autumn, but soon it'd be a winter in my life.

We turned into Earlsdon Avenue where the trees usually sang in concert at my even then youthful sky. The police car stationary outside 29. The terror was to come and it was to keep coming and still keeps coming as my day blacked out in utter, fractured despair.

The officer, kind and unassuming and differently embarrassed, led me up my crinkled anaglypta stairs. Wrapped still – and still – in his shawl was Daniel. Barely six months of life. Now gone, all silent. Distant trains, lurching towards New Street, crashed like thunder. Please wake up, my beautiful boy [B]

It happened very quickly and I really don't think there was pain at that precise moment. He just slipped quietly away, and I could feel it, life, going from him. I knew it was about to come. I think he did, in a strange and inexplicable way. He gave me a sign with his beautiful hollowed-out eyes. And I still think I saw a slight, ever so slight, turn of his head towards the light at the window, almost as if to say 'That's where I'm going'. And almost as if telling me not to worry, not to come chasing him with my heart. It was so sad. And yet I think now that it was so wonderful. That connection can never be broken [B]

He was holding me and I knew it was a special, big hold ... it was strong. Oh! Man, it was. He was holding on to me, like I was slipping away. And I wasn't, I was me and I was sad ... and lost because he'd gone ... he was my brother he'd ... we'd played footy, we'd been together, we'd done things ... and we were always together. He was crushed by his ... being sad, and I ... Fuck, I started to cry with him ... he was breathing, his breathe was all over me, it was inside, coming out ... and we were so ... wet ... in well, being sad, because that's how we felt. It's like just now, well, it's better now, but it's like yesterday. So sad. I cried for him. He's my Dad, he was our Dad, trying to protect us and yet ... he knew he'd failed I suppose, that's where the tears come from. He was there to protect us. He cried because he'd failed. He'd ... my brother ... died. Job not done, I'd say. I think that he'd have been thinking that as he was crying. And I really still feel for him in doing that. He was strong and to me all that ... doing that ... made him stronger, a big man. He is to me, and I think we're good together because of it. Because of Tez, my brother [C]

Daddy went away on a big boat that we made together. We planned it all so that he'd have a great time [C]

Themes highlighted by these fathers and sons in their narratives:

- masculinity and 'invincible' father
- struggling to understanding and find meaning in a man's way
- the importance of preparing for death
- transferring anxiety to other sons as a result of a family death

The father-and-son commentaries supporting this chapter illustrate grieving at various male life-stages. Death is visited on men and boys and the masculine response to bereavement is distinct from that of girls and women. And it is manifest in different ways and at different levels of intensity. According to bereavement specialists, there are many commonalities in the grief that fathers and sons experience, but they also recognise that individual reactions can vary and that even the same person may experience contradictory reactions at different phases of their grieving.

The death of a child has been termed 'the ultimate deprivation' (Arnold and Gemma 1983). One part of this is an inability to understand or cope with an interruption to what was hitherto accepted as incremental life-pattern in which a series of 'certainties' follow. Children are not supposed to die, and such an event leaves parents feeling disorientated. Both mother and father have to deal with two contradictory sets of feelings – on the one hand wishing that the dreadful pain they feel would evaporate and wondering if ever it will and yet knowing that their memories of their deceased child are an important part of their celebration of the abbreviated life that was lived. Both mother and father experience these feelings. The death of a child is probably the single most traumatic, devastating long-lasting experience that parents can ever encounter in their lives.

But it has been acknowledged that fathers and mothers often grieve in quite different ways. This is partly explained by the differences in the nature of the attachment between fathers and mothers and their child. At the outset the mother has the most overt and intensive bond, borne out of the emotional and physical intimacy of bearing and birthing their child and reinforced by her close involvement in providing the new-born child his immediate needs: food, warmth and physical closeness. Fathers, on the other hand, are more inclined to develop attachments gradually over time, and these are more often connected with their hopes and expectations for their child. And whilst there are changes as a result of the closer involvement nowadays of fathers in pregnancy, birth and the early child-care of their son, there remains a securely held belief that 'the father's emotional investment in parenting tends to occur later and less intensely than the mother's. This has implications for the way parents grieve' (Cordell and Thomas, 1990).

There are also important social and cultural expectations about the way fathers grieve, and this has important implications. Much of the literature on child bereavement concerns the mother, which is understandable given the attachment model highlighted above. Cook (1988), for example, states that fathers tend to approach grief from a cognitive and solitary position. The 55 men interviewed in her research regarded the effect of this as dangerous for themselves and those around them. Related to this was the presence of two additional difficulties, both of which arose from the fathers' reluctance to divulge their feelings. Firstly, an expectation by society that men should comfort their wives and other family members. Secondly, the notion, again deeply rooted in Western culture, that healthy grieving cannot be accomplished without fathers being able to the share their feelings.

As Cook maintains, this has profound implications for fathers. They continue to be viewed as the partner who has to be 'strong', showing little outward manifestation of their sense of loss. They are required by society to do this because theirs is a paternally protective function: they are there to enable the mother to grieve whilst ensuring that practical issues surrounding both the death itself and the continuation of 'life' are attended to (DeFrain, Jakub and Taylor, 1991). Horchler and Morris (1994), for example, describe fathers as 'forgotten mourners' and as 'second class grievers', their sorrow lying hidden under a range of domestic or work-related tasks – emotion is subjugated to practicality, their grief buried with their son. Commenting on this situation, Cordell and Thomas (1990) observe that 'in too many instances, fathers' responses to infant loss tend to coincide with how they believe they should act as men, rather than how they need to act to confront and resolve [their own] grief' (p.75).

This state of affairs places unrealistic expectations on fathers. There is no place or opportunity for them to grieve and it is frequently the case that their human need to grieve will surface over time and often in different ways to mothers.

Sons may be bereaved too. As with fathers, boys are often expected not to show or feel emotion and to be in a slightly better position than girls to continue with normal everyday tasks after a death (Blundell, 2002). The UK charity, *ChildLine*, captures the assumption of this male characteristic: 'My dad died this morning. They have gone round to my aunt's and I am alone with his body now.' ... 'Grandad told me what to do with his ashes but I've not been allowed to have them' (p.10).

Adolescent boys who are trying to cope with the death of their father by using essentially male coping mechanisms are struggling to do so whilst attempting to find a mature masculine identity (Blundell, *op cit*). And there are many complicating factors: a boy's ability to grieve will be influenced by his relationship with his siblings and by their gender, their deceased father's relationship with them and other family members, and by other factors – not least whether or not the father lived in the family home.

Many younger boys do cope with bereavement well. When they have a secure and loving family and an extended network of friends, they can remain 'buoyant in the face of bereavement' (Jones, 2001). It is often in adolescence that they become more aware of the finality of death and of the need to re-structure the family and take on new roles. Unresolved grief in adolescence can have damaging effects later in life; some surveys have shown that such boys are five times more likely to turn to crime, drugs or need psychiatric intervention later on in their lives (Harrington and Harrison, 1999).

The complexities of childhood or adolescent bereavement, and especially the impact on boys who lose their fathers, are only now being unravelled. Harrington and Harrington (1999) for example, argue that – contrary to widely accepted opinion – younger children who experience a family divorce are less traumatised than those who experience a parental bereavement. This appears logical since the concepts associated with death, such as finality and irreversibility, are abstractions which are clearly related to the child's cognitive development (Smilansky, 1987).

But whilst we can and should acknowledge the existence of insulating factors within the grieving process, such as the emotional status of existing family relationships, there is little doubt that boys are significant affected and that the impact is inclined to be more intense for adolescents (Worden, 1996).

This chapter has focused on the impact, differences and practical issues surrounding bereavement. We conclude this section by reinforcing the shared nature of grieving and the sense of loss that families – mothers, fathers and surviving children – all experience, by drawing on Corr's commentary:

> Despite the volumes of work on grief, the experience of grief seems to defy description ... Definitions touch the fringes of grief but do not embrace its totality or reach its core ... Grief is a complicated, evolving human process. Grief is a binding experience; its universality binds sufferers together. More is shared than is different. (Corr *et al,* 1991, p.55)

Some considerations for practitioners

Of all the events children might encounter during their school careers, bereavement is something which schools have, until very recently, been ill-prepared to deal with. Thankfully, most children do not experience the death of a parent or close family member whilst at school. But it is important to recognise that the number of pupils who experience bereavement during that time is not inconsequential. Holland (1993) pointed out that over 70 per cent of children in primary schools in Humberside had experienced the death of a parent or family member during the previous two years, and Holland and Ludford (1995) noted a similar pattern in that region's secondary schools.

Such prevalence, and the fact that children will encounter bereavement at some stage, has ensured that the theme has been identified as one of the focal points in the English government's *Healthy Schools* campaign (DoH, 2003) and also by the Scottish government (LTS, 2007). The advice and materials available through these and other agencies set out practical considerations for professionals working with children in school settings. And their advice illustrates a remarkable consistency in approach, and confirms that offered both by academic commentators (Holland, 1997) and charitable organisations (CRUSE, 2007). All note the potential dangers of children succumbing to mental health problems as a direct outcome of experiencing the death of a close family member. Readers accessing these materials will, however, note very little which is directed towards dealing overtly with the particular responses by sons or fathers to death.

Dealing in a strategic and planned way with potential or actual bereavement, incorporating considerations of gender difference, requires incorporating it within the school's in-service training portfolio. A core element should be building up knowledge and understanding of the differential impact of death and of recognising that the patterns of behaviour of bereaved boys differ significantly from those of girls. Younger boys may well display attention-seeking behaviour such as challenging or anti-social activities; adolescent boys might be inclined to suppress their response, a deflection which is consistent with male bereavement behaviour. But care should be taken not to generalise – each boy will respond in his own way.

High on a bereavement checklist for education professionals is the formulation of an overarching school policy, built on the knowledge and understanding that bereavement patterns in boys can vary, just as those of their fathers, but that whatever the differences, boys need to work through a classic process of (a) accepting loss (b) dealing with the pain of loss (c) making life adjustments which recognise the absence of a significant person and finally (d) allowing the boy to move forward in an emotionally secure way.

Schools and other education settings which have a defined policy recognised by all the adults will be better placed to deal with the way a pupil is affected by a parent's death. It is important to determine who the person or people are who can best support the boy – or the father. This person may be a member of the teaching staff, or a teaching assistant or other adult who has formed an effective emotional bond with the child. He or she will become the cornerstone for the actions which will follow. It is obviously important that, whilst schools do have a clearly articulated policy, they implement it flexibly so that practical issues surrounding death and bereavement can be managed by a named person whilst a nominated other might be identified to progress a recovery agenda. Rowling (2003) sets out a range of school-wide considerations and the *Childhood Bereavement Network* has an extensive range of resources to support professionals and parents, including a number which deal specifically with the experiences of boys and fathers specifically (see for example the wonderful *Lost Boys' Appreciation Society*; Gibbons, 2004).

13

Bad Dads, bad lads: fathers, sons and 'criminal careers'

Our house always had 'people' coming and going. It was known to the police. They lined up the pandas like taxis on a rank, just round the corner, waiting to pick local 'names' off and eating. Why do coppers in cars always eat Mars Bars? From time to time me and my mates would chuck stuff at 'em and run off ... anything, really. I remember one kid slung a chocolate milkshake across the roof of one of 'em. We laughed at the coppers, asked 'em how they liked their 'shit' car. One time they came round but didn't stop, just screamed round the corner, two cars, lights ... everything. I saw them pile in, shouting stuff and running through the house and ... came out with my Dad, who was hunched up and swearing out loud at them ... like, it was him saying, you've got the wrong man! We all must've laughed out loud because he looked across and winked. Oh yes, they'd definitely got the wrong man ... [A]

There was always a group of us at the playground's edge; largely avoided and largely avoiding each other. The mums had a sort of solidarity, their legitimacy given; the legitimate dads, too: they were taking theirs home to the concrete family. We, on the other hand, were only here Tuesdays and Thursdays – and every other week perhaps Monday mornings and Friday afternoons – and wore our guilt like a leper's bell; we kept ourselves largely to ourselves, and fawned if allowed briefly into some few words with a neighbour; were too loud, too hearty, too grateful to be spoken to. We had something of our own hierarchy, too; we certainly would have nothing to do with the man (in shorts winter and summer) with dreadlocks and a clear glaze of crack on his spent and grinning face; we could look with some relief that we had not come to this ...

The first time I went down to school in the new dispensation I spoke – or went to speak – to Adam, a GP with whose family we had shared meals, spent a day in Derbyshire, hosted stop-overs each way. He looked both furious and scared as I approached him and was silent as my own greeting ran out of words before saying – looking for all the world as if he might burst unto tears or else hit me – 'I think we'd rather not continue our relationship with you.' And then, after some seconds, perhaps overcome by a sense of his priggishness: 'If you don't mind'.

The bad dad in me grew from the bad kid I was at school. I didn't cut a Pol Pot figure in what I did at school – the omnipresence of my Dad saw to that. No, mine was a quiet badness, launched through humour and embellished by association with the core group of sharp lads who knew more the ways of the world. I clung to their words and deeds, a limpet learning how to fray the nerves of my teachers. And it was still there when as an early Dad I tested who and what my lad's teachers were and what they stood for. It was the sweeping defensiveness of the Dad who'd been done to at school, who'd got through a system because the support and commitment was there at home, mainlining expectation and fear in equal large measure to see me through the Bermuda Triangle of my school years. Did I have the right stuff to do the same? Could I be so selfless, however ill-directed that deep and unquestioning desire for me to get a 'proper' education had been? This is the acid test for some fathers but not all. Yes, I'll complain about the rights and many wrongs of the subjugated son, who had to fit those lofty aspirations maybe well beyond my means. And yes, as I must do now, I'll make capital and secure territory in my own mind to rationalise and fit that time in school with my outrage that an educated and humane society can allow inequalities to be the pillar-support for the raised aspirations on the nation's educational highway [B]

I never did owt in school ... never had to in them days, and I got on alright. You rely on your contacts, your mates. If you've got good contacts then that'll open doors, give you opportunity and that. As I say, school was a waste of time for me. I had one time, my first ... inside ... and I did some training and that's the first time I learnt anything of any use at all. Now there's no sense in it for the likes of me, none at all. I get where I am because of my own effort and stuff, nothing that I've got from college or that kind ... nah, nothing ... .Of course I'd mebbe do things different, take opportunities, do some work and get some qualifications ... but it's too late for me now ... and anyways he'll have something to take over when he's ready, mind. No education, that's me, but I'll still be leaving him a business ... he'll land on his feet. So he'll just do like I did ... he won't get put under pressure. But I think he's got brains, that lad ... he's not got that from me [B]

I'm like me Dad. Spot on. He was a bit of a ... bit difficult in ... when he was at school, and I reckon I'm just like it myself. I take after him, he's me Dad. When I was excluded it was well, random it was ... I can't say, but me Dad said nothing at all. Fuck, par for the course I think he'd be thinking himself 'Well, son, that's been me, I've done it, tee-shirt yeah ... and I'm doing OK'. I wonder if he thought ... I think he saw it as a commando course, you know, SAS and all stuff like it ... if you came out of it you'd survive, be OK and all of that. Then, it'd be alright for me, I'd be OK. It was part of what you get, me and him, part of the education. Me Dad's cool about it all, really OK ... he knows I'll join the business and he'll hand it on. Family, that's how it works ... just family [C]

My Dad has been in and out of prison for years, as long as I can remember anyway. I've got a list of places we've been to for visits. Some mad places. They treat you with contempt and that's bad ... when you realise what's going on. You notice it, I've noticed as I've got older and ... I'm doing sociology now and I'm finding out how these things work. Oh, yes, you're seen to be as bad as your Dad, almost as though you've done it. What's good is that I use all that stuff, inside prisons and what it's like, and I think that a few of the teachers connect with it, see that I'm actually gaining from it [C]

Themes highlighted by these fathers and sons in their narratives:

- socialised deviance amongst families
- subtle or overt isolation of 'non-normal' fathers
- schools as delinquent playgrounds
- paternal approval of inappropriate behaviour in school
- 'like father, like son' responses by professionals

It has been clear for decades that family continuity exists for many problem behaviours. Notable amongst the historical demonstrations of intergenerational continuity is the transference from father to son of criminal behaviour or, more generally, anti-social conduct which may or may not result in police involvement and court proceedings. For instance, Robins *et al* (1984) reported that 57 per cent of delinquent sons had a criminal father, whilst even earlier, McCord (1977) found that 29 per cent of sons with fathers who had been convicted for violent offences were themselves convicted for violence and 40 per cent of sons with fathers who had convictions for theft were convicted for theft. Nathan (2004) goes as far as to say 'like grandfather, like father, like son', to highlight the potency of this transmission cycle.

The literature cites numerous examples of such connections (Farrington, 1992; Rutter *et al*, 1997). Some studies show that where both biological and adoptive parents are criminals, 24 per cent of adopted children display criminal behaviour, compared with 13 per cent whose biological or adoptive parents are not (Robins *et al*, 1984). However, some care needs to be taken when considering this apparently powerful evidence for a genetic link: the samples in such studies are usually small, making generalisability problematic.

Other theories should be considered alongside genetic transfer, such as the influence of the family and its psychological profile. Wilson (1987) has concluded that a convicted family member was influential in the subsequent criminality of a son, rather than the structural factors such as poor housing or poverty. Farrington and West (1990) are unequivocal, stating that having a convicted father was the surest predictor of offspring offending and engaging in anti-social behaviour. Nevertheless caution should be exercised in family-based studies about the transfer of criminal behaviour between father and son, as it is difficult to isolate the causal variables (Nathan, 2004).

Attention has recently been paid to the dynamics and psychology of family interactions in the quest to identify a causal link between fathers and their sons. Again, researchers have found it difficult to isolate causal variables. Consideration has been given to family size (Farrington *et al*, 1996), social learning of delinquent behaviour (Patterson *et al*, 1989), attachment theory and rejection (McCord 1983), and to the links between child abuse and subsequent offending (Widom, 1989; Browne and Falshaw, 1998).

Closer examination of families as social units reveals illuminating information regarding 'disrupted families' and delinquency patterns. Juby and Farrington (2001), reporting on the findings of the Cambridge Study in Delinquent Development, found that the 75 boys who were living in 'permanently disrupted' families or in 'high-conflict' families showed higher rates of delinquency than those living in intact families. The study went on to explore the role of 'father closeness' as inhibiting delinquency and as an explanatory factor for maintaining socially adjusted families. The study recommends making interventions which encourage the formation and maintenance of opportunities for fathers and their children to form strong emotional and social bonds.

Ultimately, however, it seems that practitioners need to recognise the somewhat muted research evidence in support of any one theory regarding a 'cycle of offending'. Whatever the contributing factors, the father's criminality or disposition towards anti-social behaviour, or his absence from the family home, results in a far higher than average tendency towards delinquency and then criminality by his son. The problem in England and Wales is serious. In the early 1990s it was reported that over a third of men in prison had children dependent upon them – a statistic made worse when considered alongside signal failures to progress prison reform, not least education courses with emphasis on parenting. For example, the provision of parenting courses for young offenders was found to promote promising changes in their attitude and awareness towards parenthood (Caddle, 1991).

The evidence about the link between education and criminality has emerged from recent studies. Devlin (1995) used a biographical approach in securing accounts from offenders regarding their schooldays. All the evidence highlights the likelihood that offenders will have a particular profile – they will have been to several schools during their compulsory education, they will experience learning difficulties at some stage in their school career and they will mainly be drawn from socially disadvantaged homes. Moreover, Devlin's data shows that offenders will have been involved in truancy and absenteeism and they will also have particular views about their teachers and of problem behaviour in lessons. These data have a familiar ring to them, pointing to a continued cycle of underachievement and offending, in which both father and son are implicated.

Some considerations for practitioners

Such interventions as those reported by Caddle (1991) offer some cause for optimism. But they constitute, at best, a reactive intervention in young men who may well already have become part of a 'criminal class' (Devlin, 1999). Even if such initiatives were more widespread, their long-term effect might be questioned because of an established pattern of offending behaviour. Intervention strategies are required long before boys offend, and should invoke the collaboration of the relevant children's and young people's services alongside education.

If one of the precursors of delinquent or criminal activity is the problem behaviour of boys in schools – as we have highlighted – certain imperatives need to be at the forefront of educational strategy and practice. Recent English government initiatives relating to 'behaviour and attendance' have stressed the need to adopt preventative approaches geared to promoting 'positive discipline' and 'behaviour for learning' (DfES, 2003; B4L, 2004). Such approaches are built on established linkages – notably between a boy's performance as a learner in school and a predisposition to behave inappropriately.

The efficacy of such approaches in reducing offending behaviour has been dramatically illustrated by the Montreal Longitudinal Experimental Study, aimed at assessing the long-term impact and clinical significance of two-year preventive intervention programmes on criminal behaviour and academic achievement amongst boys. The study is based on a large sample (250 disruptive or aggressive boys), with a low-risk control group. Intervention was directed to three key areas:

- social skills training for the boys
- parent training in effective child-rearing
- information and support for teachers

It was found that significantly more boys in the intervention than in the control group completed high school. Their rate of criminal record was similar to that of the low-risk group. The likelihood of having a criminal record was almost twice as high for the control group as for the intervention group.

These results confirm the evidence that reducing boys' early disruptiveness prevents later educational problems and crime. At a time when professional collaboration in the multidisciplinary children's services is being developed there cause for optimism. However, it should be reiterated that 'problem boys' and their fathers, whether 'disruptive' in school or 'delinquent' outside it, are the least likely people to evoke sentiments of support or engagement from normative populations. An attitudinal shift is essential to accompany concerted multi-agency intervention.

14

'Is that your Dad?'
Fathers outside the school gates

I was ashamed to see my Dad at school. There was one time, one event when I was mortified, we were going to Summer Camp, this was the School Scouts, the School Scout Troop, and we were going oh about twenty or thirty miles away to a camp near Garstang, I think, and they'd written to all the parents asking for volunteer Dads with cars to lift us and my Dad came. I mean that was unusual for a start because he had nothing to do with school or scouts, I mean he didn't have much to do with us really. Anyway he turned up in his van, his work van. He was a plumber and there's like this shabby old van, a Ford Escort which he'd painted himself and you could see that, with 'D.G*****, Plumber and Heating Engineer' on it and all these other Dads with Jags and Mercs and – no really, I mean it was that sort of school [Boys' Independent Grammar] you know? And there he was and they were standing around in like sweaters and slacks, if you know what I mean and he very wasn't in sweaters and slacks and he just stood to one side with that sneer of his because like no one was talking to him and I was aware that, I was aware of that and I think part of me was sort of sorry for him but I think a bigger part of me was deeply ashamed and squirming you know? And part of me was like looking at him through those others' eyes and he was, I mean there he was this little shabby dirty working-class man with his sneer and I just wanted to die ...

Actually there was just one other time when he was working near school I was about 12, 13 perhaps and he offered to give me a lift to school instead of going on the bus and he drove right up the school drive – this was I don't know about 120 yards, like a football-pitch length – and he dropped me off in the van, and everybody's walking up this drive and I have to get out, don't I, right in front of the Masters' Quad [Car Park] and I died, I was burning. And the next day when he offered I said I had to be in early for a Chess Club meeting or something yeh? And I went out at half-past six and sat in the park for two hours before I went [to school] but he knew, I'm sure he knew. He didn't say anything but he knew [A]

I was very much aware that I was one of few boys in the school whose dad wasn't a professional, medic, accountant, lawyer whatever. I suppose that can't have been strictly true but I think everybody else's dad was either professional or had a business in the town and there were a lot of Jewish kids whose dads commuted into Manchester and the whole place was really up itself like that and my dad was a plumber, no but wait, wait! My younger brother went to Q****'s School too and – wait! – in his fifth year they did like this survey in General Studies about class, social class, and Jeff was the only – the only! – boy in this class of twenty-odd who was real WC! No, wait, and he had to stand up and talk about it! It's true, he did! He had to give a short talk about his family background, I don't mean whether there was coal in the bath or anything but like what his dad did, and what they ate and where they took holidays. It's true, I tell you, and this was in about 1965, I mean not that long ago. Would you believe it?

... I don't know, I'll never know, will I? I mean whether I was just a little snob or whether it was something to do with him; I mean he was ... awful. He was, he was a horrid man. I tell you what, I remember there was a kid in our class ... Harper? David Harper I think, and he was just so proud of his dad, and his dad was a carpenter or joiner or something and Harper did puppet shows and one end-of-term you know when you can read books or do puzzles or whatever, Harper put on a show and his dad came and ... transported the stage set, the puppet show and set it up, and watched and he was so proud and Harper was so proud and proud of his dad you could see ... and the rest of the class were secretly taking the piss out of Harper Senior he had his overalls on and he spoke lahk that, tha' knows – well not really but a real East Lancs twang – and I joined in. I joined in ... [A]

My Dad dressed well, immaculately really. He had escaped his New Mills overalls, though I note that even then the photographic evidence said that he'd look smart if he'd worked as a lifeguard slurry farm: collar and tie, razor-creased overalls which were surely fresh each day. And shoes, now there's an inheritance: shoes that would blind you if the other son shone. An escape into a proper job was for him a passport to an even more embellished pride in appearance. I think he stood out at parents evenings, other school events. It is possible that this was compensation, because the only thing to announce his presence was his immaculate appearance: he never seemed to talk the talk of men in groups, exchanging worried news and commentaries about world situations, life and football. Maybe he did, but I can never recall it. Silent father, silent son. I'm sure he must have said things, at least, that's what I'd like to think, rather than to acquiesce to the unquestionable knowledge and status of Mr Regan, who's got a BSc 'with honours, you know, look ... ' and like the other teachers '... must know a thing or two'. He had a great sense of achievement, deep down, I'm sure, which was not going to be betrayed by arriving at anything closely associated with my school in anything other than his 'best' clothes. He was unable to portray the relaxed confidence of someone who was comfortable with who he was. I think he always felt that he had something to prove. And to be fair, in those days schools did very little to promote a shared approach – looking back the teachers it seems to me even now were 'in charge'. Dads like mine were so grateful that their sons had achieved, made it [A]

I sometimes feel strange, you know ... a bit out of place. I feel that I don't exactly fit in, waiting there for the lad to come out. All those mums seems to have such a lot in common, chatting, laughing ... and I feel awkward about starting up a conversation with anyone. I don't think it's just me [B]

I get called on to help out, with the music, drama and stuff like that ... well, you'd expect that, wouldn't you? But I don't think I fit in especially [B]

I love it when Dad comes in. It's good giving ... I put arms around him, Dad, it feels ... it's nice to do it. Not many Dads stand outside ... waiting for us. Some boys go straight up to their Mums and don't say ... they don't tell them much and it is just like usual, Mums are there all the time ... But when your Dad's there it's ... it's ... you run to them and hold them, holding on to them, getting hold of them to say to yourself that 'He's really here, he is really ... yes ... he's really here' [C]

Most of the time its my mum who comes (to school) but it's special ... good ... when Dad comes down, because ... he always brings things for us, it makes me feel ... big ... better, a bit ... And I always ask him 'Will you be coming to school today?', and if he is I have a nice feeling inside me waiting for the bell and looking out for him. We run up to him and you smell his cigarettes but ... we don't mind, it's his smell [C]

Themes highlighted by these fathers and sons in their narratives:

- feelings of embarrassment (sons), awkwardness (fathers)
- strong sense of 'place' and identity with fathers by sons
- feelings of being marginalised
- fathers are conscious of status, linked to employment
- competition amongst sons ('my dad's better than yours')
- at KS 1 and 2, boys like to be met by their fathers

As fathers we have stood in often splendid isolation outside the gates of primary schools, waiting for our sons to appear. It feels uncomfortable, and it is exactly that. Fathers at the school gates are frequently excluded, probably unintentionally, from the intricacies and intimacies of mothers' talk. We never really know the territory, the people and especially the movers and shakers and gossip pedlars. Such is the penalty for many employed fathers of episodic attendance. Of course, there are dads who are able, for whatever reason, to be constant in attending these and other gatherings. And many others feel comfortable in their role as occasional participant, interacting easily with mothers: but mainly the picture is one of matriarchal dominance at the school gates. Indeed, one recent report (*Fathers Direct*, 2007) states that 'school life is dominated by women'.

This position is reinforced by entrenched traditional attitudes to childcare. Fagan and Palm (2004) report that many workers in nursery settings believe that they meet mainly mothers. The reality, however, is that far more fathers than is recognised are involved in nursery or school drop-offs or pick-ups. Burgess and Bartlett (2004) come to the same conclusion, observing that most early years practitioners hear the word 'parent' as 'mother' – a common response amongst parents too.

But fathers themselves carry with them a range of misconceptions, beliefs and histories. Many come to an educational setting with an abiding sense of having been a failure at school. Some bring their son to school because currently they are reluctantly unemployed: their own self-esteem and confidence may well be low (Burgess, 2006). So they retreat from socialising with other parents. And it is also important to factor in a masculine response-style to social encounters, which might present initially as reserved, preoccupied or disinterested.

Involving fathers in the important ephemera that comprise the school run is a major organisational and attitudinal challenge for schools, as well as challenging the perceptions of a good many fathers. Yet fathers indicate that they appreciate involvement in activities which, although often beyond the classroom, can be important components of their son's learning and socialisation.

Relatively little research, however, directly relates to the views of fathers who encounter these situations and feel intimidated by them. We found it as difficult to trace accounts of this phenomenon as we did to trace teaching dads (see Chapter 7). So we have again resorted to a small group – four fathers whom we asked for their views about some of the generic observations in this chapter. Their comments provide a fascinating glimpse into the present negative reality for fathers who wait outside the school gates. And it indicates what might be done to address their feelings of marginalisation and otherness.

One of the dads, David, summarised how many fathers feel. He encapsulates both their sense of isolation and defeat at their lack of recognition as a parent: '*Sometimes I go there and feel quite unusual really. It's a bit like I'm the invisible man ... yes, because I suppose I'm the only bloke and all these girls, mothers are busy talking to each other. And I'm pretty sure they'd be there talking about a lot of the stuff that I'd be wanting to talk about as a father or as a mother. I've thought sometimes of not going up to collect him*'.

These feelings are reinforced by another dad: '*There were a couple of the mothers that I'd talked to a bit, but not all that much. I still don't really see myself as included in stuff like coffee mornings or anything of that sort*' (Iain).

The net effect of schools which don't offer a positive message about fathers is to give them a sense of retreatism, which is often rationalised by barely credible explanations to the parents who are part of the social circle of the school gate. As Salim remarked: '*I purposely don't go up to people. I don't want to be seen as a weirdo or someone who's not got any friends*', a statement which was the more poignant because he was one of only five non-white fathers in a semi-rural primary school.

Although four fathers cannot provide a representative view, Tony's words are a fair summation of what anecdotal or little research-based evidence exists about this issue: '*The school ought to do more to put us in there where it counts. I think they should be much more active ... but, well, it's not surprising is it if the school is just about 100 per cent women? Us Dads, we're strangers*'.

Iain, however, made a proactive response to his own perceptions of feeling marginalised. He told us that '*The best thing I did was bring our new Labrador pup to school on the times I was collecting Sean. Its funny how something as neutral ... non problematic sort of, like a dog can ... be a bridge into chatting with people. After that you've got a point of connection to fall back on*'.

Some considerations for practitioners

Elsewhere in this book we have identified some of the strategies schools can adopt to make them both father- and boy-friendly. A crucial factor is to communicate to fathers that the school recognises them as partners (alongside the mother) in the education of their son. The creation of a father-friendly ethos involves as much action outside the classroom as inside. One way in which this can be done is by checking the messages conveyed to all parents by the displays, notices and organisation of the entrance area or foyer of the school. As this is the usual point of entry for parents on school business, it can be a focal point for visual clues to tell fathers that they are welcome and valued in the school.

Attention also needs to be given to the attitudes and perceptions of all staff. What are their beliefs about men in general and about fathers in particular? Are they as comfortable talking to fathers as to mothers? Comments along the lines of 'Are you being mum today?' are, to say the least, unhelpful role-stereotype reinforcements. Staff should also work on strategies to engage fathers directly when they come in to school to drop off or pick up their sons. Such issues need to be discussed with care and facilitated by specialist professionals.

The Children's Plan has confirmed the core importance of fathers in the academic and social development of their sons (DCSF, 2007) and has at national level initiated strategies which have been advocated for many years by pressure groups and organisations representing fathers. It remains to be seen whether professional cultures and hierarchies in education, particularly the early years and primary schooling, are so deeply gendered as to maintain the isolation of fathers from the task of educating boys.

15
Young fathers

My Mum and Dad ... that was tough, really bad and I felt so, so uncool 'cos, well, I'd been ... I think I was ... they felt I was , I knew things ... and it was me ... I was so this and so that, I knew everything, lots of girls, you know, I was ... enjoying being me, a kid ... young. And they thought I was all sorted, knew stuff ... you know what I'm saying, birds and bees and things and I came across ... I was the kid who was just so cool and ... well, in control, I was sorted. Kids, mates, came to me ... to our house, because they weren't sure, needed boosting up, needed ... So it came as a big shock and ... errm ... it was big, real big ... I remember Mum going off and ... well, I knew she'd be off with a tear, crying because she'd, well, I'd left her ... become a man. It was bad, that time ... it wasn't good. My Dad, well, he was just ... quiet, taking it all in. I kept thinking, I wonder when he's going to sound off. But he never did [A]

Dad was a young Dad, so it didn't come as any surprise to him at all. I think he just thought of it as natural, really. Two uncles were the same, they all had kids in their teens, and their girls were much younger even than them. So it runs in the family. I had enough to think about too, and so I was pleased that he was cool about it. He even dipped in for some baby stuff, pram, clothes and all that, so it was a help too [A]

There's part of me now still thinking, and then even more I think ... saying that my lads got the old man in him, you know. Attractive kid, she was nice and he was ... well, I'd say ... I'd have said then, a bit out of his league ... yeah, she was smart alright. I was in his shoes I reckon, thought well, you would I'd say, that'd be me ... So, no. I wasn't pissed off at all, not a bit.

He was 17, yeah? I'd do the 'ruining your life' one, that's got to happen, most Dads would do it I reckon, just give 'em the line. But I was, deep down ... Well, I was chuffed to be honest, my lad and that ... I was going to be a Grand-dad, me, and I'm still in full flow, in the middle of my life. I was OK about it. I was really OK [B]

It's good. Really, really good. Me and Kelly, we're sound and it's brought us together because there's something there that we need to look after, both of us. It's ... like, when you're little you feel there should be somebody ... caring, looking for you you, making sure there's ... .um ... no danger and that. You expect it 'cos you're young and ... well, I did that I felt that my sister ... oh, that was in primary school, that was ... long time ago, really ... but she did ... and, that's what you do, when you're a Dad. You get those feelings, like ... in reverse, sort of thing ... .so that I'm now really doing it ... caring, looking after, being ... well, I don't know, but he's mine and Kelly's and we'll look out for him. That's what being a Dad is, that's what happens ... [B]

I got trapped ... she trapped me and ... it was her being ... needing to be wanted, 24/7. I think she thought, 'Yeah, I'll have a kid, and then I've got him'. But it didn't work with me and I've got mates who've done the same too ... when your girl does that stuff you ... well it's an instinct and that's what you do. When it happens to mates you see 'em getting lower and lower, sort of ... sinking, sucked down by it all and ... You think about it and all the stuff that you do which is good and it just gets in the fucking way, that stuff ... Oh, well, I did have a try ... I tried to do it, be the ... be ... coming back in, regular doing the ... we did go, used to go shopping, Tesco's, the food stuff and ... I saw ... you could tell that people were thinking things, saying things like ... you know, kids, and being a weight ... not being ... just, well, you could tell in their fucking faces, yeah, that's it ... But it was ... well, I was really down then because I knew I was trapped and I began to hate the kid for taking stuff away from me ... I did ... I still ... well ... a bit of me still feels that, it's true ... I still think, fuck, she tricked me there, and now I'm paying ... well, I would be if I was there [B]

My Dad's the youngest Dad in our school I'd say. I like it, because he's quite trendy and sporty ... not like others who are pretty crusty ... so I think it's good ... it makes me feel good because I'm not embarrassed when he comes into school ... you know, he's not got a big belly or bad teeth, he's pretty cool you know, so ... [C]

Dad is still at college. He is very clever, and my Mum likes him a lot. She's older but not as clever as him. I like it a lot when Dad is at home because I get to play with him. He's got lots of friends and they're at college too [C]

Themes highlighted by these fathers and sons in their narratives:

- coping responses of fathers and their sons
- influence of family birth traditions
- resilience factors in successful young fathering
- range of young fathers – negative and positive perspectives
- advantages of being a young dad

Young men – adolescents – who become fathers comprise a dichotomous population. They are at once the most at risk of becoming social problems or even casualties, and yet invisible in the face of overriding societal concerns (Ferguson and Hogan, 2004). The preoccupation of post-industrial western nation-states has typically been directed towards the problems – mainly the social costs – of young mothers (Vera Institute of Justice, 1990). This seems to be paradoxical and a needlessly gendered situation. Young mothers need, in an overt and utilitarian sense, fathers. Evans (2001) has reported the influence on young mothers of the views of their baby's father when deciding on whether to abort their pregnancy or proceed to full term. And the perceptions of young mothers towards their pregnancy has been shown to be significantly influenced by the positive views of the baby's father towards a forthcoming birth (Hellerstedt *et al*, 2001).

It is frequently pointed out that an abiding misconception is that 'young' mothers are partnered in the conception of their child by 'young' fathers – in other words, adolescent mothers = adolescent fathers. In the United States, Beymer (1995) dispelled this myth by reviewing national statistics for that country, finding that about 70 per cent of all adolescent or 'teen' mothers had partners – the father of the child – who were at least 20 years of age. According to Beymer there is consequently much misconception about teenage fathers; they are '... the victims of massive misunderstanding'.

The early life stories of young mothers and young fathers overlap (Bunting and McAuley, 2005). Young fathers are characterised by low economic status, correspondingly low attainment levels in school, and by rather poor knowledge about contraception. Moreover, there are significant correlations between young fatherhood and anti-social behaviour and substance abuse (Pears *et al*, 2005). And Tan and Quinlivan (2006) have recently identified an association between early fatherhood and the exposure of the father to domestic violence in his early childhood and to his exposure to drug usage.

Part of the difficulty in looking at the challenges faced by young fathers relates to the difficulty of identifying a definitive population. Sonenstein (1986) has long been used to illustrate the problem of identifying a secure and accurate estimate of the proportion of young fathers because many of them are not listed on birth registration forms. However, about 30 per cent of children born to teenage mothers are estimated to be sired by teenage males (Beymer, 1995).

Adolescent fathers face particular problems. Whilst fathers as a gendered community are subject to stereotype and misgiving, younger fathers encounter an additional spectrum of societal assumptions regarding their role (Kiselica, 1995). They certainly face very real difficulties. These include depression and anxiety (Achatz and MacAllum, 1994), conflict issues concerning decisions surrounding abortion or adoption (Robinson, 1988) and tensions between the young father and the mother and her family, often characterised by denial of access to the child (Kiselica *et al*, 1992). Young fathers also face major question-marks over their competence as fathers, an issue not aided by the general invisibility of the issue ((Hendricks, 1988).

Moreover, adolescent fathers face specific education or education-related difficulties. Not least of these is their tendency to drop out of school before statutory leaving-age (Furstenberg, Brooks-Gunn and Chase-Lansdale, 1989) and consequently have problems in securing employment. Achatz and MacAllum (1994) refer to the way in which the lives of young fathers are often characterised by long-term career dissatisfaction and financial hardship. The potential, and in many cases real, social isolation that such conditions can generate are compounded by the shifts in the relationship of young fathers with their immediate peers.

Young fathers, therefore, present a particular set of phenomena. They appear to be marginalised by their lifestyle choice – if it is indeed a choice – by public perception and by the impact of low economic opportunity, social isolation and an understandable inability to cope with new responsibility. And whilst charitable and mandatory networks operate for young teenage mothers, there are few such facilities for young fathers.

One misconception amongst the many that are held about young fathers is that they are indifferent about being involved in the pregnancy and the upbringing of their child (Bunting and McAuley, 2005). Some commentators (for example, Florsheim and Ngu, 2003) have further noted that involvement in fathering a child was for some a wake-up call for disadvantaged adolescent boys, who used – whether or not wittingly – the event to make major changes in their lives.

Some considerations for practitioners

Most schools now have extensive, 'wrap around' systems for the emotional and physical support of pupils, including specific arrangements for those who are involved in teenage pregnancy. Far more such initiatives are directed towards the girls. The need to provide information and support for teenage fathers has been slower to materialise. Nevertheless, there has been a significant increase in the last ten or so years in the attention directed towards boys who become fathers whilst they are still in school.

One important hurdle to be overcome relates to a commonly held perception that teenage boys *de facto* become reluctant fathers. This is not always so. Moreover, there is a tendency for non-professionals (i.e. those not working directly with young fathers in health-related professions) to make assumptions about the lifestyle choices of young parents. This is especially pertinent because the professional gatekeepers most young fathers encounter may well have followed more traditional parenting pathways, as professional women and men tend to defer parenthood.

Fathers who are in school need to be insulated from innuendo and scapegoating by other pupils and regrettably – although this is rare – by some adults working in schools. All these responses need to be countered by information-sharing. Non-specialist professionals therefore need systematic and informed guidance on a range of pregnancy-related issues: physiology, nurturing behaviour, the differential emotional responses by boys to becoming a father, the impact of the pregnancy cycle on schoolwork, and so on. And they need to act positively as non-judgemental sources of information: there must at least be a procedure to enable a young expectant father to secure such information quickly and without feelings of embarrassment or marginalisation.

Examples of successful programmes dedicated to supporting teenage fathers are now more numerous: the resources section of this book lists some sources of information. Two such examples, quoted by an *Engaging Fathers* publication (DfES, 2004) can be taken from The Health Initiatives Team at Education Leeds and the *Ladz 2 Dadz* project in Northamptonshire. Both initiatives have shown that successful and productive engagement with school-age fathers can foster positive outcomes for young fathers and their children.

Useful resources for fathers and sons

When researching this book we were reassured by the range and volume of support materials available for fathers and their sons. They come in various forms: printed materials, internet-based resources or face-to-face opportunity for discussion and support. Many of these resources are accessible in community languages. We have accessed each of these materials during the course of writing this book. The list below contains some which have a national focus and others with a more international flavour:

Parentline Plus Advice for dads and mums
0808 800 2222 (24 hr helpline)
www.parentlineplus.org.uk

Centre for Separated Families Supporting dads and mums
01904 610321
www.separatedfamilies.org.uk

Families Need Fathers
Advice for separated fathers from dads who have gone through it
Tel 08707 607496 (6pm-10pm)
www.fnf.org.uk

Family and Parenting Institute
Charity providing resources for fathers (and mothers)
http://www.familyandparenting.org

Fathers.Com
US website of the National Centre for Fathering
http://www.fathers.com

Fathers Direct
National Information Centre on Fatherhood
www.fathersdirect.com

Fathers First
General advice and helpline for fathers
www.fathersfirst.org

Fathering Project
Reporting research on fathers in Western Australia
www.thefatheringroject.org

Gingerbread
Advice for lone dads and mums
0800 018 4318)
www.gingerbread.org.uk

National Family and Parenting Institute
Reports and booklets
020 7424 3460
www.nfpi.org

NZ Father and Child Society
Web resource with content for specifically for fathers
http://www.fatherandchild.org.nz/index.htm

Sure Start
Information about local services for parents
0800 096 0296
www.surestart.gov.uk

Teachersfirst
US website with good section dedicated to fathers
http://www.teachersfirst.com/fathers.html

Success for Boys
Australian Government initiative to improve boys' learning outcomes
http://www.dest.gov.au/sectors/school_education/policy_initiatives_reviews/key-issues/boys_education/

References

Achatz, M. and MacAllum, C. (1994) *Young unwed fathers: Report from the field.* Philadelphia: Public/Private Ventures.

Ackerman, R. (1993) *Silent Sons: a book for and about men.* New York: Simon and Schuster.

American Psychiatric Association (2000) *Diagnostic and Statistical Manual of Mental Disorders (DSM-IV).* Washington DC: APA.

Aries, P. (1962). *Centuries of Childhood: a social history of family life.* New York: Vintage Books.

Arnold, J. and Gemma, P. (1983) *A Child Dies: a portrait of family grief.* Rockville, MD: Aspen Systems Corporation.

Audit Commission (1999) *Missing Out.* London: The Audit Commission

Avon Longitudinal Study of Parents and Children (2006) Bristol: University of Bristol

Ballard, K. (1994) *Disability, Family, Whānau and Society.* Palmerston North, NZ: Dunmore Press.

Barnett, D., Hunt, K., Butler, C., McGaskill, J., Kaplin-Estrin, M. and Pipp-Siegal, S. (1999) 'Indices of attachment disorganization among toddlers with neurological and non-neurological problems', in J. Solomon and C. George (eds) *Attachment Disorganisation.* New York: The Guilford Press.

BBC News (2005) 'Will fathers' involvement improve education?' http://news.bbc.co.uk/1/hi/talking_point/4414111.stm (accessed 21 November, 2007)

Behaviour for Learning (2004) www.behaviour4learning.ac.uk (accessed 3 October, 2007)

Beymer, L. (1995) *Meeting the guidance and counselling needs of boys.* Alexandria, VA; American Counseling Association.

Bloom-Feshbach, J. (1981) 'Historical Perspectives on the Father's Role', in M. Lamb (ed.) *The Role of the Father in Child Development.* New York: Wiley.

Blundell, S. (2002) 'Fatherless Sons: Psycho-analytical psychotherapy with bereaved boys', in J. Trowell and A. Etchegoyen (eds.) *The Importance of Fathers: A Psychoanalytic Re-evaluation.* London: Institute of Psycho-Analysis.

Boisjoli R, Vitaro F, Lacourse E, Barker E and Tremblay R (2007). Impact and clinical significance of a preventive intervention for disruptive boys: 15-year follow-up. *British Journal of Psychiatry*, 191, 415-419.

Bowlby, J. (1951) Childcare and the Growth of Love. Harmondsworth: Penguin.

Bridges, D. (1987) 'It's the ones who never turn up that you really want to see: the problem of the non-attending parent', in J. Bastiani (ed.) *Parents and Teachers.* Slough: NFER.

Brighouse, T. (1985) 'The idea of the school: the expectations of parents, teachers and children' in C. Cullingford (ed.) Parents, Teachers and Schools. London: Robert Royce

British Educational Research Association (2004) *Revised Ethical Guidelines for Educational Research.* Southwell: BERA.

Bronfenbrenner, U. (1975) 'Ecology of child development'. *Proceedings of the American Philosophical Society,* 119, 439-469.

Browne, K. and Falshaw, L. (1998) 'Street children and crime in the United Kingdom: a case of abuse and neglect'. *Child Abuse Review* 71-13.

Bunting, L. and McAuley, C. (2004) 'Teenage pregnancy and parenthood: The Role of Fathers'. *Child and Family Social Work*, 9 (3), 295-303.

Burgess, A. (2006) 'Engaging Fathers in their Children's Learning: tips for practitioners' http://www.fathersdirect.com/index.php?id=12andcID=323 (accessed 29 October, 2007)

Burgess A and Bartlett D (2004) *Working with Fathers: a guide for everyone working with families.* London: Fathers Direct

Burgess, A., and Ruxton, S. (1996) *Men and their children: Proposals for public policy.* London: Institute for Public Policy Research

Caddle, D. (1991) *Parenthood training for Young Offenders: an evaluation of courses in Young Offender Institutions.* London: Home Office

Caldwell, C., Antonucci, T. and Jackson, J.(1998). Supportive/conflictual family relations and depressive symptomatology: Teenage mother and grandmother perspectives. *Family Relations*, 47(4), 395-402

Carpenter, B., Addenbrooke, M., Attfield, E. and Conway, S. (2004) 'The needs of fathers with disabilities', *British Journal of Special Education*, 31 (2), 75-80.

Carpenter, B. and Herbert, E. (1997) 'Fathers: are we meeting their needs?', in B. Carpenter (1997) (ed.) *Families in Context. Emerging Trends in Family Support and Early Intervention.* London: David Fulton Publishers.

CBBC (2007) 'What do you think of sports day?' (http://news.bbc.co.uk/cbbcnews/hi/chat/your_comments/newsid_3039000/3039827.stm) (Accessed 11 November, 2007)

Centre for the Child Care Workforce and Human Services (2002) *Estimating the size and components of the US child care work-force and care giving population: key findings from the child care workforce estimate (preliminary report).* Washington, DC and Seattle, WA: CCCW.

Chandler, T. (1997) 'Daring to care – men and childcare', in M. Whalley (ed.) *Working with Parents*. London: Hodder and Stoughton.

Childhood Bereavement Network (2007) (http://www.childhoodbereavementnetwork.org.uk/index.htm) Accessed 12 December, 2007.

Childline (2003) *Boys allowed. What boys and young men tell Childline about their lives.* London: Childline

Coley, R. and Medeiros, B. (2007) 'Reciprocal longitudinal relations between non-resident father involvement and adolescent delinquency'. *Child Development*, 78, 132-147.

Cook, J. (1988) 'Dad's double binds .Rethinking Fathers' Bereavement from a Men's Studies Perspective'. *Journal of Contemporary Ethnography*,17 (3), 285-308

Cordell, A. and Thomas, N. (1990) 'Fathers and Grieving: Coping with Infant Death'. *Journal of Perinatology*, 10 (1).

Corr, C., Fuller, H., Barnickol, C. and Corr, D. (Eds.). (1991) *Sudden Infant Death Syndrome: Who Can Help and How.* New York: Springer Publishing Company, Inc.

DeFrain, J., Jakub, E. and Taylor, J. (1991) *Sudden Infant Death Syndrome: Enduring the Loss.* Lexington, MA: Lexington Books.

Corrigan, P. (1979) *Schooling the Smash Street Kids.* Basingstoke: Macmillan.

Cox, A. and Lambrenos, K. (1992) 'Childhood physical disability and attachment', Development Medicine and Child Neurology, 34, 1037-1046.

Crockenberg, S. and Leerkes, E. (2005) 'Infant Social and emotional development in Family Context', in C. Zeanah (ed.) *Handbook of Infant Mental Health.* London: The Guilford Press.

Crozier, G. and Reay, D. (2005) (Eds.) *Activating Participation: parents and teachers working towards partnership.* Stoke-on-Trent: Trentham Books

Cunningham, B. and Dorsey, B. (2004) 'Out of site but not out of mind'. *Child Care Information Exchange*, 165, 42-43.

Day, C., Kington, A., Stobart, G. and Sammons, P. (2006) 'The Personal and Professional Selves of Teachers: Stable and Unstable Identities. *British Educational Research Journal*, 35(4), 601-616.

Day, R., Lewis, C., O'Brien, M. and Lamb, M. (2005) 'Fatherhood and father involvement: emerging constructs and theoretical orientations', in V. Bengston, A. Acock., K. Allen, P. Dillworth-Anderson and D. Klein (eds.) *Sourcebook of Family Theory and Research.* Thousand Oaks, CA: Sage.

Department for Children Schools and Families (2007) *The Children's Plan: Building a Brighter Future.* London: DCSF.

Department of Children, Schools and Families (2007) *Permanent and Fixed Period Exclusions from Schools and Exclusion Appeals in England 2005/06* at http://www.dfes.gov.uk/rsgateway/DB/SFR/s000733/index.shtml (accessed 14 January, 2008)

Department for Children, Schools and Families (2007) *The Children's Plan.* London: DCSF.

Department for Education and Employment (1998) *Meeting Special Educational Needs. A programme of Action.* London: DfEE.

Department for Education and Skills (2001) E*very Child Matters.* London: DfES

Department for Education and Skills (2002) *Extended Schools: providing opportunities and services for all.* London: Department for Education and Skills.

Department for Education and Skills (2003) *Behaviour and Attendance Strategy (KS3 and 4).* London: DfES.

Department for Education and Skills (2006) *First Statistical Release.* London: DfES

Department for Education and Skills and Department of Health (2003) *Using the National Healthy School Standard to Raise Boys' Achievement.* LondonL DfES/DoH.

Department of Health (2005) Healthy Schools. http://www.healthyschools.gov.uk/Default.aspx (accessed 19 November, 2007)

Deven, F. (1994) *Men, Media and Childcare. European Commission Network On Childcare.* Brussels: European Commission

Devlin, A. (1995) *Criminal Classes.* Winchester: Waterside Press.

Douglas, J. (1964) *The Home and the school. A Study of Ability and Attainment in the Primary School.* London: Panther Books.

Eaves, L., Heath, A., Martin, M., Maes, H., Neale, M., Kendler, K., Kirk, K. and Corey, L. (1999) 'Comparing the biological and cultural inheritance of personality and social attitude in the Virginia 30,000 study of twins and their relatives'. *Twin Research*, 2, 62-80.

Egan-Sage, E. and Carpenter, J. (1999) 'Family characteristics of children in cases of alleged abuse and neglect'. *Child Abuse Review*, 8 (5), 301-313.

Equal Opportunities Commission (2002) *Fathers and the Modern Family.* London: Equal Opportunities Commission.

ESRC (2006) Findings from the Peterborough Youth Study at http://www.scopic.ac.uk/documents/Peterborougharticle_000.pdf (accessed 27 October, 2007)

ESYTC (2003) *The Edinburgh Study of Youth Transitions and Crime*, at http://www.law.ed.ac.uk/cls/esytc/newssummer_2003.htm (accessed 27 October, 2007)

Evans, A. (2001) 'The influence of significant others on Australian teenagers' decisions about pregnancy resolution'. *Family Planning Perspectives*, 33 (5), 224-230.

Fagan, J. (1996) 'Principles for developing male involvement programs in early childhood settings: a personal experience'. *Young Children*, 51 (4), 64-71.

Fagan, J. (1999) *Predictors of father figure involvement in pre-kindergarten Head Start.* Philadelphia, PA: University of Pennsylvania, National Center on Fathers and Families.

Fagan, J. and Iglesias, A. (1999) 'Father involvement program effects on fathers, father figures, and their head start children: a quasi-experimental study'. *Early Childhood Research Quarterly*, 14 (2), 243-269.

Fagan, J. and Palm, G. (2004) *Fathers and Early Childhood Programs.* New York: Delmar Learning

Family and Parenting Institute (2006) *Moving on: how to be an involved father.* London: FPI

Farrington, D. (1992) 'Trends in English juvenile delinquency and their explanation', *International Journal of Comparative and Applied Criminal Justice*, 16, 151-163.

Farrington, D. (1995) 'The Development of Offending and Antisocial Behavour from Childhood: Key Findings from the Cambridge Study in Delinquent Development', *Journal of Child Psychology and Psychiatry*, 36 (6), 929-964.

Farrington, D., Barnes, G. and Lambert, S. (1996) 'The concentration of offending in families'. *Legal and Criminological Psychology*, 1, 47-63.

Farrington, D. and Jolliffe, D. (2005) 'Crime and Justice in England and Wales, 1981 – 99' in T. Michael and D. Farrington (eds.). *Crime and Punishment in Western Countries.* Chicago: University of Chicago Press, pp. 41 – 82.

Fein, R. (1978) 'Research on fathering: Social policy and an emergent perspective'. *Journal of Social Issues*, 34, 122-135.

Feinstein, L. and Symons, (1999) Attainment in secondary school. *Economic Papers,* 5, 300-321

Feldman, S., Nash, S. and Aschenbrenner, B. (1983) 'Antecedents of Fathering', *Child Development,* 54, 1628-1636.

Ferguson, H. and Hogan, F. (2004) *Strengthening Families through Fathers: developing policy and practice in relation to vulnerable fathers and their families.* Dublin: DSFA.

Fisher, K., McCulloch, A. and Gershuny, J. (1999) 'British fathers and children', unpublished report, available at http://wwww.iser.essex.ac.uk

Fletcher, R. and Dally, K. (2002) *'Fathers' involvement in their children's literacy development.* Newcastle: The Family Action Research Centre at the University of Newcastle, Australia.

Florsheim, P. and Ngu, L. (2003) Differential outcomes amongst adolescent fathers: understanding fatherhood as a transformative process. Paper presented at the Rocco C. and Marion S. Siciliano Forum Mini Conference, October 18.

Flouri, E., Buchanan, A., Welsh, E. and Lewis, J. (2004) *Father's Involvement with Their Secondary-Aged Children. Summary of Findings.*

Frater, G. (1997) *Improving Boys' Literacy.* London: The Basic Skills Agency.

Freud, S. (1923) *The ego and the id.* London: Hogarth.

Furstenberg, F., Brooks-Gunn, J. and Chase-Lansdale, J. (1989) 'Teenaged pregnancy and childbearing'. *American Psychologist,* 44, 313-420.

Furstenberg, F. and Harris, K. (1993). 'When and why fathers matter; Impacts of father involvement on the children of adolescent mothers'. In R. Lerman and T. Ooms (Eds.) *Young unwed fathers: Changing roles and emerging policies.* Philadelphia: Temple University. (pp. 117-138).

Gavidia-Payne, S. and Stoneman, Z. (2004) 'Family predictors of maternal and paternal involvement in programmes for young children with disabilities.' in: M. Feldman (ed.) *Early Intervention: The essential readings.* Oxford: Blackwell.

Gibbons, A. (2004) *Lost Boys' Appreciation Society.* London: Orion Children's Books

Goldman, R. (2004) *Fathers' Involvement in Children's Education: A Review of Research and Practice.* London: National Family and Parenting Institute.

Goodacre, E. (1968) *Teachers and their Pupils Home Background.* Slough: NFER.

Hurt, J. (1985) 'Parental involvement in schools: a historical perspective', in C. Cullingford (ed.) *Parents, Teachers and Schools.* London: Robert Royce.

Green, S. (2003) 'Involving fathers in family literacy: Outcomes and Insights', from the 'Fathers Reading Every Day' program. *Family Literacy Forum and Literacy Harvest,* Fall, 34-40 (available at www.lacnyc.org accessed 16 October, 2007)

Hadadian, A. (1995) 'Attitudes towards deafness and security of attachment relationships amongst young deaf children and their parents', *Early Education and Development,* 6, 181-191.

Hareven, T. (1971) 'The history of the family as an interdisciplinary field'. *Journal of Interdisciplinary History,* 2, 399-414.

Harrington, R and Harrison, L. (1999) 'Unproven assumptions about the impact of bereavement on children'. *Journal of the Royal Society of Medicine,* 92, 230-233.

Harris, C (1994) *Emasculation of the unicorn: The loss and rebuilding of masculinity in America.* York Beach ME: Nicolas-Hays.

Hassall, R. and Rose, J. (2005) 'Parental Cognitions and Adaptations to the Demands of Caring for a Child with an Intellectual Disability: A Review of the Literature and Implications for Clinical Interventions', *Behavioural and Cognitive Psychotherapy,* 33, 71-88.

Hellerstedt, W., Fee, R., McNeely, C., Sieving, R., Shew, M. and Resnick, M. (2001) 'Pregnancy feelings amongst adolescents awaiting pregnancy test results'. *Public Health Reports,* 116, 180-193

Hendricks, L. (1988) 'Outreach with teenage fathers: A preliminary report on three ethnic groups' *Adolescence* 23, 711-720.

Hines, D. and Saudino, K. (2006) 'Gender Differences in Psychological, Physical, and Sexual Aggression Among College Students Using the Revised Conflict Tactics Scales.' *Violence and Victims* 18, 197-217.

Hirshberg, L. and Svejda, M. (1990) 'When infants look to their parents: Infants' social referencing of mothers compared to fathers'. *Child Development,* 61, 1175-1186.

Hobcraft, J. (1998) *Childhood experience and the risk of social exclusion in adulthood. Centre for the Analysis of Social Exclusion.* London: LSE.

Hobcraft, J. (1998) *Intergenerational and Life-Course Transmission of Social Exclusion: Influences of Childhood Poverty, Family Disruption, and Contact with the Police.* London: LSE.

Hodges, J. and Tizard, B. (1989) 'Social and family relationships of ex-institutional adolescents'. *Journal of Child Psychology and Psychiatry,* 30, 77-97.

Holland, J. (1993) 'Child bereavement in Humberside primary schools'. *Educational Research,* 35 (3)

Holland, J. (1997) *Coping with Bereavement.* Cardiff: Cardiff Academic Press.

Holland, J. and Ludford, C. (1995) 'The effects of bereavement on children in Humberside secondary schools'. *British Journal of Special Education*, 22 (2).

Home Office (1991) *Criminal and Custodial careers of those born in 1953, 1958 and 1963. Home Office Statistical Bulletin, 1989b.* London: The Home Office.

Home Office (2003) National Statistics (available at http://www.statistics.gov.uk/cci/nugget.asp?id=1101). Accessed 22, October 2007

Horchler J.. and Morris, B. (1994) *The SIDS Survival Guide: Information and Comfort for Grieving Family and Friends and Professionals Who Seek to Help Them.* Hyattsville, MD: SIDS Educational Services.

Jones, H. (2001) *Bibliotherapy for Bereaved Children.* London: Jessica Kingsley.

Hostler, P. (1953) *The Child's World.* London: Benn.

Howe, D. (2005) 'Disabled children, parent-child interaction and attachment', *Child and Family Social Work*, 11, 95-106.

Hymowitz, K. (1999). *Ready or Not: Why Treating Children as Adults Endangers Their Future and Ours.* New York: The Free Press.

Jackson, B. (1984) *Fatherhood.* London: Allen and Unwin.

Jackson, D. (1998) 'Breaking out of the binary trap: boys = underachievement, schooling and gender relations'. In D. Epstein, J. Elwood, V. Hey, and J. Maw (eds) *Failing Boys?, Issues in gender and achievement.* Buckingham: Open University Press.

Jaffee, S., Caspi, A., Moffitt, T., Taylor, A. and Dickson, N. (2001) 'Predicting early fatherhood and whether young fathers live with their children: prospective findings and policy considerations'. *Journal of Child Psychology and Psychiatry*, 42, 803-815.

Jolliff, D. and Horne, A. (1999) 'Growing Up Male. The Development of Mature Masculinity', in A. Horne and M. Kiselica (eds.) *Handbook of Counseling Boys and Adolescent Males.* Thousand Oaks CA: Sage Publications.

Juby, H. and Farrington, P. (2001)'Disentangling the Link between Disrupted Families and Delinquency Sociodemography, Ethnicity and Risk Behaviours', *The British Journal of Criminology*, 41, 22-40 .

Kahn, T. (2006) *Involving Fathers in Early Years Settings: Evaluating Four Models for Effective Practice Development.* Report prepared for the Department for Education and Skills. London: Pre-School Learning Alliance.

Kidzworld (2007) 'Violence in Sports – Parents Behaving Badly' (http://www.kidzworld.com/article/5591-youth-sports-violence) (Accessed 11 November, 2007)

Kiselica, M. (1995) *Multicultural counselling with teenage fathers: A practical guide.* Thousand Oaks CA: Sage.

Kiselica, M., Stroud, J., Stroud, J. and Rotzien, A. (1992) Counseling the ?????

Kitzinger, S. (1988) *Freedom and Choice in Childbirth.* London: Penguin.

Klinnert, M. (1984) 'The regulation of infant behavior by maternal facial expression'. *Infant Behavior and Development*, 7, 447-465.

League, S. and Ford, L. (1996) 'Fathers' Involvement in Their Children's Special Education Program'. Paper to the annual Meeting of the National Association of School Psychologists. Atlanta GA, March 15.

Learning and Teaching in Scotland (2007) http://www.ltscotland.org.uk/index.asp (accessed 19 November, 2007)

Lee, K. (2005) 'Fatherhood across the life course: paternal careers and generational change'. Paper presented to the CRFR Conference for New Researchers in Families and Relationships. 25 October.

Lewis, C. and Lamb, M. (2007) *Understanding Fatherhood.* York: Joseph Rowntree Foundation.

Lloyd, T. (1999) *Reading for the future: Boys' and father's views on reading.* London: Save the Children.

Lupton, D. and Barclay, L. (1997) *Constructing Fatherhood: Discourses and Experiences.* London: Sage.

Marsiglio, W., Day, R. and Lamb, M. (2000) 'Scholarship on fatherhood in the 1990s and beyond', *Journal of Marriage and the Family*, 62, 1173-1191.

Martin, C., Cabrol, S., Bouvard, M., Lepine, J. and Mouren-Simeoni, M. (1999) 'Anxiety and Depressive Disorders in Fathers and Mothers of Anxious School-Refusing Children'. *Journal of the American Academy of Child and Adolescent Psychiatry.* 38 (7), 916-922.

Martino, W. and Meyenn, B. (eds.) (2001) *What About The Boys? Issues of Masculinity in Schools.* Buckingham: Open University Press.

McBride, B. and Rane, R. (2001) 'Father/Male Involvement in Early Childhood Programs: Training Staff to Work with Men', in J. Fagan and A. J. Hawkins (eds) *Clinical and Educational Interventions with Fathers.* Binghampton, NY: The Haworth Clinical Practice Press

McBride, B. Rane, R. and Bae, J. (2000) 'Intervening with Teachers to Encourage Father/Male Involvement in Early Childhood Programs'. *Early Childhood Research Quarterly*,16, 77-93.

McConkey, R. (1994) 'Early intervention: planning futures, shaping years'. *Mental Handicap Research*, 7 (1), 4-15.

McCord, J. (1977) 'A comparative study of two generations of Native Americans'. In: R. Meier (Ed.) *Theory in Criminology.* California: Sage.

McCord, J. (1983) 'A forty-year perspective on effects of child abuse and neglect'. *Child Abuse and Neglect*, 7, 265-70.

McLanahan, S., and Booth, K. (1989). Mother-only families: Problems, prospects, and politics. *Journal of Marriage and the Family*, 51, 557-580.

McShane, G., Walter, G. and Rey, J. (2001) 'Characteristics of adolescents with school refusal'. *Australian and New Zealand Journal of Psychiatry*, 35 (6), 822-826.

Meyer, D. (1986) 'Fathers of handicapped children', in R. Fewell and P. Vadasy (eds.) *Families of handicapped children.* Austin, TX: Pro-Ed

Minnes, P. (1998) 'Mental retardation: The impact upon the family', in J. Burack, R. Hodapp and E. Ziegler (eds.) *Handbook of mental retardation and development.* New York: Cambridge University Press, pp. 693-712.

Mumme, D., Fernald, A. and Herrara, C. (1996) 'Infant's responses to facial and vocal emotional signals in a social referencing paradigm'. *Child Development*, 67, 3219-3237.

Nathan, G. (2004) 'Crime and the family: like grandfather, like father, like son?' *British Journal of Forensic Practice*, December, 2004

National Foundation for Educational Research (1995) *Attitudes to Schooling.* Slough: NFER

National Foundation for Educational Research (2004) *Annual Survey of Trends in Education.* Slough: NFER

NCOFF (National Centre on Fathers and Families) (1999) *Predictors of Father and Father Figure Involvement in Pre-Kindergarten Head Start.* Phildadelphia: University of Pennsylvania/NCOFF.

Nord, C., Brimholl, D. and West, J. (1997) *Fathers involvement in their children's school.* Washington, DC: U.S. Department of Education, National Center for Education Statistics.

Office for Standards in Education (2001) *Improving Attendance and Behaviour in Secondary Schools.* London: Ofsted

Parke, R. and Tinsley, B. (1987) 'Family interaction in infancy'. In J. Osofsky (ed) *Handbook of Infant Development.* New York: Wiley.

Patterson, G., DeBaryshe, B. and Ramsey, E. (1989) 'A developmental perspective on antisocial behaviour'. *American Psychologist*, 44 (2), 329-35.

Pattman, R., Frosh, S. and Phoenix, A. (1998) 'Lads, Machos and Others'. *Journal of Youth Studies*, 1, 125-142

Pears, K., Pierce, S., Kim, H., Capaldi, D. and Owen, L. (2005) 'The timing of entry into fatherhood in young, at-risk men'. *Journal of Marriage and the Family,* 67 (2), 429-447.

Pittman, F. (2006) Fathers and Sons. *Psychology Today* pp.1-3

Pleck, J. (1971) 'The male sex-role: Definitions, problems and sources of change', in J. Williams (ed.) *Psychology of women: selected readings.* New York: Norton.

Pleck, J. and Masciadrelli, B. (2004) 'Paternal involvement by US resident fathers: levels sources and consequences', in M. Lamb (ed.) *The Role of the Father in Child Development.* Chichester: Wiley.

Pollack, W. (1998) *Real Boys: Rescuing our sons from the myths of boyhood.* New York: Henry Holt.

Power, T. and Parke, R. (1983) 'Patterns of mother and father play with with their 8 month old infant: a multiple analyses approach'. *Infant Behavior and Development*, 13, 391-395.

Quinton, D., and Rutter, M. (1988). *Parenting breakdown: The making and breaking of inter-generational links.* Aldershot: Avebury

Ramchandani, P., Stein, A., Evans, J., and O'Connor, T. (2005) 'Paternal depression in the postnatal period and child development: a prospective longitudinal study'. *The Lancet*, June 25.

Razwan, S. (2000) *Fathers' Involvement in their Children's Upbringing and Education: A Study of experiences of fathers and children in the Thornbury and Bradford Moor areas of Bradford.* London: The Children's Society.

Robins, L., Mednick, B., Gabrill, W. and Hutchings, B. (1984) Genetic influences in criminal convictions. Evidence from an adoption cohort. *Science* 244 981-4.

Robinson, B. (1988) *Teenage Fathers.* Lexington, Mass:D.C. Heath and Company.

Roffey, S. (2002) *School Behaviour and Families.* London: David Fulton Publishers.

Rogers, C. (2007) 'Disabling a family? Emotional dilemmas experienced in becoming a parent of a child with learning disabilities', *British Journal of Special Education*, 34 (3), 136-143.

Rowling, L. (2003) *Grief in School Communities: effective support strategies.* Buckingham: Open University Press

Rutter, M. (1997) 'New Cycles of Disadvantage'. Lecture to the New Cycles of Disadvantage Conference. ESRC Centre for Analysis of Social Exclusion (CASE). Stoke Rochford, Grantham, 27-28 November.

Rutter, M. and Madge, N. (1976) *Cycles of Disadvantage.* Heinemann: London

Sanders, K. (2002) 'Viewpoint: Men don't care?' *Young Children*, 57 (6), 44-48.

Rutter, M., Maughan, B., Meyer, J., Pickles, A., Silberg, J., Simonoff, E. and Taylor, E. (1997) 'Heterogeneity of antisocial behaviour: Causes, continuities and consequences', in D. Osgood (Ed.) *Nebraska symposium on motivation (Vol. 44) Motivation and delinquency.* Lincoln, NE: University of Nebraska Press. pp 45-118.

Sandow, S. and Garner, P. (1994) 'Saints, Fools and Gaolors? A New Role of Special Educators' in I. Lawrence (ed) *Education Tomorrow.* London: Cassell.

Seligman, M. and Darling, R. (1997) *Ordinary Families, Special Children: a systems approach to childhood disability.* New York: The Guilford Press.

Sewell, T. (1996) *Black Masculinities and Schooling.* Stoke-on-Trent: Trentham Books

Sheline, J. , Skipper, B. and Broadhead, E. (1994) 'Risk factors for violent behaviour in elementary school boys: Have you hugged your child today?' *American Journal of Public Health*, 84, 661-663.

Shipman, K. and Hicks, K. (2001) *How can Teachers Motivate Less Motivated Boys?* Slough: NFER.

Sikes, P. (1985) 'The Life Cycle of the Teacher', in S. Ball and I. Goodson (eds) *Teachers' Lives and Careers.* Lewes: The Falmer Press

Skidmore, C. (with The Bow Group) (2007) *Boys: A School Report.* London: The Bow Group.

Smart, C. and Stevens, P. (2000) *Cohabitation Breakdown.* London: Family Policy Studies Centre.

Smilansky, S. (1987). *On death: Helping children understand and cope.* New York: Peter Lang.

Smith, J. (1995) 'The First Intruder. Fatherhood, a historical perspective', in P. Moss (ed.) *Father Figures. Fathers in the families of the 1990s.* Edinburgh: HMSO.

Social Care Institute for Excellence (2005) 'Being a father to a child with disabilities: issues and what helps' (SCARE Briefing Report 16). [Online at: www.scie.org.uk]

Sonenstein, F. (1986) 'Risking paternity: Sex and contraception among adolescent males. In A. Fisher and M. Lamb. (eds.) *Adolescent fatherhood.* Hillsdale, NJ: Lawrence Erlbaum.

Speak, S., Cameron, S. and Gilroy, r. (1997) *Young Single fathers: Participation in Fatherhood – Bridges and Barriers.* London: Family Policy Studies Centre.

Spielberg, W. (1999) 'a Cultural Critique of Current Practices of Male Adolescent Identity Formation', in A. Horne and M. Kiselica (eds.) *Handbook of Counseling Boys and Adolescent Males.* Thousand Oaks CA: Sage Publications.

Stearns, P. (1979) *Be a man! Males in modern society.* New York: Holmes and Meier.

Steele, H., Steele, M., Croft, C. and Fonagy, P. (1999) 'Infant-mother attachment at one year predicts children's understanding of mixed emotions at six years', *Social Development,* 8, 161-178.

Susman-Stillman, A., Kalkoske, M., Egeland, B. and Waldeman, I. (1996) 'Infant temperament and maternal sensitivity as predictors of attachment security'. *Infant Behavior and Development,* 19, 33-47.

Tan, L. and Quinlivan, J. (2006) 'Domestic violence, single parenthood, and fathers in the setting of teenage pregnancy'. *Journal of Adolescent Health,* 38 (3), 201-207.

Trust for the Study of Adolescence, The (2007) *Supporting Young Fathers Network* http://www.youngfathers.net/contacts/service_providers.htm (accessed 14 September, 2007)

Vadasy, P., Meyer, D., Fewell, R. and Greenburg, M. (1985) 'Supporting fathers of handicapped young children: Preliminary findings of programme effects'. *Analysis and Intervention in Developmental Disabilities,* 5, 151-163

Vera Institute of Justice (1990) *The male role in teenage pregnancy and parenting; New directions of public policy.* New York: Vera Institute of Justice.

Vincent, C. (2000) *Including Parents? Education, citizenship and family agency.* Buckingham: Open University Press.

Volling, B., Herrera, M., Notaro, P. and McElwain, N. (1998) 'Differences and similarities in maternal and paternal emotion socialization: Effects on infant affect and attention'. Paper presented to the Biennial Conference on Infant Studies, Atlanta, April.

Wardle, F. (2004) 'The challenge of boys in our early childhood programs', *Earlychildhood NEWS,* 16(1) 16-21.

Wardle, F. (2007) 'Men in Early Childhood: Fathers and Teachers' *Early Childhood News.* http://www.earlychildhoodnews.com/earlychildhood/article_view.aspx?ArticleID=400n (Accessed 29 October, 2007)

Weare, K. and Gray, G. (2003) *What Works in Developing Children's Emotional and Social Competence and Wellbeing?* Research Report 456. London: DfES

Welsh, E., Buchanan, A., Flouri, E. and Lewis, J. (2004) *Fathers' involvement with their secondary-school-aged children.* London: National Children's Bureau

Welshman, J. (2006) *Underclass: A History of the Excluded, 1880-2000.* London: Continuum.

West, S. (2000) *Just a Shadow: A review of support for the fathers of children with disabilities.* Birmingham: The Handsel Trust.

West, P. and Herjanic, B. (1975) 'Arrests and delinquency in two generations: a study of black urban families and their children'. *Journal of Child Psychology and Psychiatry* 16 125-40.

Whalley, M. (2003) 'Developing evidence-based practice', in M. Whalley and the Pen Green Centre Team (eds.) *Involving Parents in their Children's Learning.* London: Paul Chapman Publishing.

Whitehead, J. (2004) Jack Whitehead's Writings. http://people.bath.ac.uk/edsajw/writing.shtml (Accessed on 9 January, 2008)

Widom C (1989) 'Child abuse, neglect, and violent criminal behaviour'. *Criminology*, 27, 251-71.

Willis, P. (1977) *Learning to Labour.* Aldershot: Gower

Wilson, H. (1987) 'Parental supervision re-examined'. *British Journal of Criminology.* 27, 275-301.

Worden, J. (1996) *Children and Grief: When a parent dies.* New York, NY: Guilford Press.

Wright, C., Weekes, D. and McGlaughlin, A. (2000) *'Race', Class and Gender in Exclusion from School.* London: Falmer Press

Young Voice (2005) *Parenting Under Pressure: Prison.* London: Young Voice.

Zimmerman, M., Salem, D. and Notaro, P. (2000). 'Make room for daddy II: The positive effects of fathers' role in adolescent development', In R. Taylor and L. Wang (eds.), *Resilience across contexts: Family, work, culture, and community.* Mahwah, NJ: Lawrence Erlbaum Associates, Inc.

Zimmerman, M., Steinman, K. and Rowe, K. (1998). Violence among urban African-American adolescents: The protective effects of parental support. In S. Oskamp and B Arriaga (eds.) *Addressing Community Problems: Research and Intervention.* Newbury Park, CA, Sage.

Zucker, K. and Bradley, S. (2005) 'Gender Identity Disorder', in C. Zeanah (ed.) *Handbook of Infant Mental Health.* London: The Guilford Press.

Index